T0220751

Adaptive Interaction

A utility maximization approach to understanding human interaction with technology

Synthesis Lectures on Human-Centered Informatics

Editor
John M. Carroll, *Penn State University*

Human-Centered Informatics (HCI) is the intersection of the cultural, the social, the cognitive, and the aesthetic with computing and information technology. It encompasses a huge range of issues, theories, technologies, designs, tools, environments and human experiences in knowledge work, recreation and leisure activity, teaching and learning, and the potpourri of everyday life. The series will publish state-of-the-art syntheses, case studies, and tutorials in key areas. It will share the focus of leading international conferences in HCI.

Adaptive Interaction: A utility maximization approach to understanding human interaction with technology
Stephen J. Payne and Andrew Howes
2013

Making Claims: Knowledge Design, Capture, and Sharing in HCI
D. Scott McCrickard
2012

HCI Theory: Classical, Modern, and Contemporary
Yvonne Rogers
2012

Activity Theory in HCI: Fundamentals and Reflections
Victor Kaptelinin and Bonnie Nardi
2012

Conceptual Models: Core to Good Design
Jeff Johnson and Austin Henderson
2011

Geographical Design: Spatial Cognition and Geographical Information Science
Stephen C. Hirtle
2011

User-Centered Agile Methods
Hugh Beyer
2010

Experience-Centered Design: Designers, Users, and Communities in Dialogue
Peter Wright and John McCarthy
2010

Experience Design: Technology for All the Right Reasons
Marc Hassenzahl
2010

Designing and Evaluating Usable Technology in Industrial Research: Three Case Studies
Clare-Marie Karat and John Karat
2010

Interacting with Information
Ann Blandford and Simon Attfield
2010

Designing for User Engagement: Aesthetic and Attractive User Interfaces
Alistair Sutcliffe
2009

Context-Aware Mobile Computing: Affordances of Space, Social Awareness, and Social Influence
Geri Gay
2009

Studies of Work and the Workplace in HCI: Concepts and Techniques
Graham Button and Wes Sharrock
2009

Semiotic Engineering Methods for Scientific Research in HCI
Clarisse Sieckenius de Souza and Carla Faria Leitão
2009

Common Ground in Electronically Mediated Conversation
Andrew Monk
2008

© Springer Nature Switzerland AG 2022

Reprint of original edition © Morgan & Claypool 2013

All rights reserved. No part of this publication may be reproduced, stored in a retrieval system, or transmitted in any form or by any means—electronic, mechanical, photocopy, recording, or any other except for brief quotations in printed reviews, without the prior permission of the publisher.

Adaptive Interaction: A utility maximization approach to understanding human interaction with technology

Stephen J. Payne and Andrew Howes

ISBN: 978-3-031-01071-2   paperback
ISBN: 978-3-031-02199-2   ebook

DOI 10.1007/978-3-031-02199-2

A Publication in the Springer series
SYNTHESIS LECTURES ON HUMAN-CENTERED INFORMATICS

Lecture #16
Series Editor: John M. Carroll, *Penn State University*
Series ISSN
Synthesis Lectures on Human-Centered Informatics
Print 1946-7680   Electronic 1946-7699

Adaptive Interaction

A utility maximization approach to understanding human interaction with technology

Stephen J. Payne
Department of Computer Science, University of Bath

Andrew Howes
School of Computer Science, University of Birmingham

SYNTHESIS LECTURES ON HUMAN–CENTERED INFORMATICS #16

ABSTRACT

This lecture describes a theoretical framework for the behavioural sciences that holds high promise for theory-driven research and design in Human-Computer Interaction. The framework is designed to tackle the adaptive, ecological, and bounded nature of human behaviour. It is designed to help scientists and practitioners reason about why people choose to behave as they do and to explain which strategies people choose in response to utility, ecology, and cognitive information processing mechanisms. A key idea is that people choose strategies so as to maximise utility given constraints. The framework is illustrated with a number of examples including pointing, multitasking, skim-reading, online purchasing, Signal Detection Theory and diagnosis, and the influence of reputation on purchasing decisions. Importantly, these examples span from perceptual/motor coordination, through cognition to social interaction. Finally, the lecture discusses the challenging idea that people seek to find optimal strategies and also discusses the implications for behavioral investigation in HCI.

KEYWORDS

HCI theory, cognitive science, bounded optimality, information foraging

Contents

Preface

Many colleagues and students have helped us to develop the ideas in this lecture, over many years. Their names appear as co-authors with one or both of us on many cited papers. In particular, we would like to thank: Duncan Brumby, Geoffrey Duggan, Stelios Lelis, Richard L. Lewis, Hansjoerg Neth, Will Reader, Kenton O'Hara, Satinder Singh, and Alonso Vera.

We would additionally like to thank the series editor, Jack Carroll, and our Morgan Claypool contact, Diane Cerra, for fantastic support and especially patience. Russell Beale and Alan Dix provided invaluable comments on the penultimate draft.

Where sections of this lecture are based strongly on our own empirical work, we have sometimes drawn substantially on published papers with these co-authors. These sources are of course cited at the appropriate junctures, but we want additionally to draw attention to them here: Duggan & Payne (2009), Duggan & Payne (2011), Howes et al. (2009), Lelis & Howes (2008, 2011), S. J. Payne et al. (2001), S. J. Payne et al. (2007), Reader & Payne (2007).

Stephen J. Payne and Andrew Howes
February 2013

Figure Credits

Figure 4.1   Based on Stephens, D. W., & Krebs, J. R. (1986). *Foraging theory*. Copyright © 1986, Princeton University Press: Princeton, New Jersey.

Figure 6.1, 6.2, 6.3   From Howes, A., Lewis, R.L. and Vera, A. 2009. Rational adaptation under task and processing constraints: Implications for testing theories of cognition and action. *Psychological Review*, Volume 116(4), 717-751. Copyright © 2009, American Psychological Association. Used with permission.

Figure 8.1   From Reader, W.R. and Payne, S.J. 2007. Allocating time across multiple texts: Sampling and satisficing. *Human-Computer Interaction*, Volume 22(3), 263-298. Copyright © 2007, Taylor and Francis. Used with permission.

CHAPTER 1

Introduction: A Framework for Cognitive Science Research on HCI

Our aim is to describe and promote a theoretical framework for the behavioural sciences that holds high promise for theory-driven research and design in Human-Computer Interaction. The framework, called *Adaptive Interaction*, is designed to tackle the adaptive, ecological, and bounded nature of human behaviour. It is designed to help scientists and practitioners reason about why people interact with computers as they do. While it has most often to date been applied to somewhat abstract tasks, we argue it has the potential to answer questions in HCI that range from low-level questions concerning, for example, button design to higher-level questions concerning design for mediated social and collaborative interaction. We illustrate the framework with examples that include a model of how long it takes to select a button that is adaptive to the cost of error (it is not Fitts's Law!) and models of the role of trust in online purchasing decisions. In each example we describe how observed behaviours emerge as an adaptation to a combination of utility, ecological experience, and information processing bounds.

The framework (Figure 1.1) derives its explanatory power from the assumption that the discretionary strategies that underpin human behaviour are determined through utility maximisation given the combination of *ecology*, *utility*, and information processing *mechanisms* available to the individual. In other words, the space of strategies that an individual will select is delineated by the ecology (as it is experienced by an individual), their internal subjective utility function, and by the cognitive mechanisms that allow them to process information. Interaction is adaptive because it is driven by strategies that are constrained by these three components. The promise of the framework hinges on the idea, which is illustrated in Figure 1, that all three components are required to predict the strategies that people will adopt. In the absence of any one component a theory is incomplete, the strategy space is unbounded, and explanation of behaviour much harder.

The potential contribution of Adaptive Interaction to HCI is exciting to the extent that it can provide the theoretical framework that is so urgently needed to guide and organise HCI research. A number of HCI researchers have made a call to theory (Y. Rogers, 2011; Dourish, 2004). This call is motivated in part by the extraordinary diversity of design challenges that HCI research faces. Much of the need for new theory has been driven by the opportunities that mobile, ubiquitous, and socially mediating technologies provide. It has also been driven by the observation that people

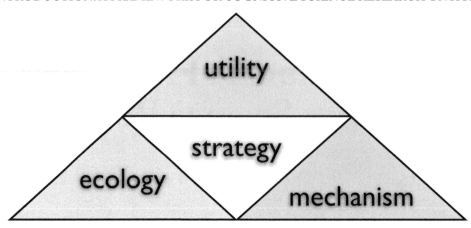

Figure 1.1: An illustration of the Adaptive Interaction framework. There are four components that are critical to understanding human interaction with technology. Utility concerns what a person wants to do, i.e., in what they find value. It defines the currency of interaction; how a person trades quantities that are physiologically, cognitively, or socially meaningful. Ecology concerns the constraints imposed by a person's interaction with, and experience of, their environment, including the immediate local task environment and the environment experienced through a lifetime. Mechanism concerns the information processing system implemented in the human brain that determines what a person can do. The first three components (utility, ecology, mechanism) shape the fourth: the choice of strategies which are discretionary methods for achieving useful behaviour. In the absence of any one of the first three components, the strategy space is unbounded.

work in teams, that technologies are used for entertainment as well as work, that social context is of overwhelming value to people. As a consequence, any one area of the behavioural sciences, whether it is psychology, sociology, economics, or management science seems, individually, inadequate as a basis of a framework for HCI. However, we believe that Adaptive Interaction which has roots across these disciplines, is sufficient to rise to this challenge.

At first sight Adaptive Interaction may appear unpromising because, despite its breadth, it has particularly strong roots in cognitive science, which has been the source of persistent dissatisfaction within the HCI community. The criticism has been aimed at the mentalistic, quantitative, rationalistic, and representational commitments of cognitive science for HCI (Dourish, 2004; Suchman, 1987). However, the real problem, we argue, is manifest in the extent to which cognitive science for HCI, and, in fact, HCI more broadly, fails to address the *adaptive* nature of human interaction with technology. The real failure of HCI-theory, whether it is cognitive science, distributed cognition, embodied cognition, situated action, or activity theory is that it has failed to provide a genuinely predictive, cumulative, and explanatory account of *adaptation*.

A theory of adaptive interaction needs to address this deficit in cognitive science for HCI but it also needs to embrace the following signature phenomena of HCI.

1. *People are adaptive to the internal resources available for computation* Information can be stored in the head or it can be stored in the world (S. J. Payne et al., 2001; Howes & Payne, 1990; Howes, 1993, 1994; Y. Rogers & Brignull, 2003; Gray & Fu, 2001; Gray et al., 2006). Computation, for example planning, can be performed in the head or it can be performed in interaction with the world (O'Hara & Payne, 1999, 1998). Exactly what can be stored and computed in the head is limited by the cognitive-neural systems of the mind and people adapt behaviour to bounds imposed by these mechanisms. For example, the known limitations of human memory impose severe limits on how easily procedures can be remembered. As a consequence, people may encode strategies for information retrieval rather than put effort into encoding information in the mind (Dix et al., 2003; Sparrow et al., 2011).

   Some researchers assume that the presence of psychological bounds mean that people try to offload as much work as possible on to the world. Advocates of *distributed cognition* have, for example, proposed that a general principle of cognitive systems is that "people off-load cognitive effort to the environment whenever practical" (Hollan et al., 2000, p. 181), and that artefacts and representations should be designed to maximize the potential for such off-loading (Zhang & Norman, 1994; Y. Rogers & Brignull, 2003). Ballard et al. (1997) refer to the minimal memory hypothesis. For example, it is assumed that the more that a cockpit can do by way of "remembering its speed," automating stall monitoring, or sounding alarms, then the less that a pilot will do. However, as we will see in Section 9 the evidence actually suggests that people distribute information processing to the environment only to the extent that it allows them to make adaptive use of their internal processing capabilities. People adaptively distribute cognition (S. J. Payne et al., 2001). People do not try to minimise effort, they do not try to minimise the use of cognitive resources, rather they try and use these resources adaptively.

2. *People are adaptive to context* (Dourish, 2004; Hutchins, 2010; Y. Rogers, 2011; Lave, 1988). In fact, many researchers believe that context is so overwhelmingly important in determining interactive behaviour, and differences between contexts are so great, that a paradigm shift is required in theories of interaction towards the phenomenological, qualitative, ecological, and embodied (Heath & Luff, 1992; Dourish, 2004; Hutchins, 2010; Y. Rogers, 2011). Such a change goes hand-in-hand with studying interaction in the wild rather than in the laboratory. The received wisdom is that information processing theories, with their perceived focus on disembodied, internal, planning, and representation are at best insufficient, at worst irrelevant, for addressing the complex problems of everyday activity.

   Consider the following examples of the effect of context on behaviour. (1) Shoppers in a grocery store figure out best buys by finding products in simple ratios, e.g., 2:1, rather than using the unit price (e.g., if product A cost $5 for 5 oz and product B cost $9 for 10 oz then a relatively easy value calculation could be made) (Lave, 1988). (2) Pilots set the position of bugs on analogue displays so as to achieve target flight speeds without remembering them (Hutchins & Lintern, 1995). (3) Information workers point to physical locations to refer to previous conversations, illustrating the potential benefit of persistent physical context for project teams (Olson & Olson, 2000).

All of these examples indicate subtle adaptations to the resources that are available in a particular context and, by implication, ways in which the disruption of the physical context by poorly thought through new technologies can have negative consequences. Even the structure of language can be adapted to the requirements of a local task environment (Garrod & Doherty, 1994). Also, detailed in-situ studies of collaborative activities reveal findings such as that London Underground controllers rarely communicate directly, preferring instead to observe each other and act accordingly (Heath & Luff, 1992), presumably avoiding interruption because of the high pressure demands of the particular context. Controllers even seem to design their work environment, orienting themselves appropriately, so as to allow observation of each other.

Lastly, it is sometimes not the physical or communicative context that matters so much as the social context (Dourish, 2004). For example, what a person chooses to post on Facebook, as opposed to say face-to-face, is shaped by their expectations of who is in the audience. Absence of awareness of online social context, and therefore a failure to make appropriate adaptations, is one factor that is known to lead to social tensions (Binder et al., 2009, 2012). In all of these cases, the context provides resources to which people shape the activity. Sometimes they even reshape the context, endogenously, so that it better supports required activities.

It has been proposed that the best way to understand the impact of the changing physical and communicative contexts of human activity is to study and record real world human activities with sociological methods. This idea (Heath & Luff, 1992) has had a deep and positive impact on HCI design practice. Arguably it is the single idea that most pervasively shapes HCI as a research discipline. Further, it has been proposed that the best way to tackle the social context for design is to abandon the "rational, empirical, scientific tradition" (Dourish, 2004, p. 20) in favour of *phenomenological* approaches that put emphasis on the subjective and qualitative experience of people in everyday life. We argue instead for a form of explanation that embraces both (1) HCI's and sociology's observation of the importance of context and (2) the scientific method.

3. *People are adaptive to utility.* Utility is a concept that has influenced many aspects of the behavioral sciences and it has a number of definitions (Bentham, 1789; Kahneman & Tversky, 1979; Fehr et al., 2008; Neumann & Morgenstern, 1947). One way to think about utility is as the subjective value of some state to a person or organism. Arguably this definition is related to notions of intrinsic motivation and reward (Bruner, 1961; Singh et al., 2010). People can anticipate the utility of future states of the world, including internal mental states and they may choose strategies on this basis. If they are utility-maximising then they will choose strategies

so as to maximise their best estimate of the cumulative anticipated utility of future states. The utility of states may be a good indicator of their value for fitness but it may not be. It may be the case that people choose to adopt utility functions that are bad for fitness, though in this case a substantial explanatory problem arises. Utility functions typically asymptote so that, for example, the value of another unit of money diminishes with wealth (Kahneman & Tversky, 1979). People can choose subjective utilities for time and money, which are sometimes thought of as efficiency concerns, but also for ethical, political, and social reasons (Fehr et al., 2008). The exact forms of the utility functions adopted by people and their consequence for behaviour are questions that are the subject of scientific investigation. Utility functions have been used for many years in HCI and Human Factors models of human interaction where their role in constraining the adaptive choice of methods has been recognised (Baron & Kleinman, 1969; Norman, 1983; Moray et al., 1991; Erev & Gopher, 1999; Howes et al., 2004; Eng et al., 2006; M. R. Smith et al., 2008; Janssen et al., 2011). Utility functions are also the subject of recent investigations using empirical techniques designed to discover the relative utility of interface designs using Mechanical Turk (Toomim et al., 2011).

Intuitively it may seem absurd that, for example, when aimlessly browsing the web, or choosing to skim Facebook, a person's behaviour can be explained as maximizing some utility function. These, after all, are well known as displacement activities; they are things that we do in place of more important tasks that we *should* be doing, tasks that bring in financial remuneration, tasks that keep a to-do list under control, tasks that mean we can finish work and relax. However, it is entirely plausible that the educational, social, and community benefits of these types of activities—activities that are systematically devalued in everyday conversation—are represented, if not consciously, in the subjective utility functions that guide human behaviour. Indeed, such a hypothesis is explored in many game theoretic approaches to understanding collaboration and also ethics (e.g., Fehr et al., 2008; Nowak & Sigmund, 2005). The possibility that skimming and browsing might be explained as utility maximizing is further explored in Section 4.

In summary, people adapt to social and physical contexts, and they simultaneously adapt to their cognitive capacities and to their subjective sense of utility. We contend that all three of these factors, as illustrated in Figure 1.1, must be accounted for in an adequate framework for understanding HCI. Adaptive interaction provides such a framework. It is a framework within which adaptations to *context* can be understood as phenomena that are simultaneously driven and limited by subjective notions of value, or *utility*, and the *mechanisms* of the mind.

Interaction may be partly hierarchical, situated, embodied, and distributed but the key principles for organising theory in HCI concern the adaptive nature of the brain's strategy selection mechanisms. In the next section we review contributions to the assumptions that underpin this claim.

CHAPTER 2

Background

The key elements of the framework have been articulated in slightly different ways by authors coming from different disciplines and traditions. In particular, the framework is explicit in Optimal Foraging Theory (Stephens & Krebs, 1986), Cognitive Game Theory (Erev & Gopher, 1999), and Cognitively Bounded Rational Analysis (Howes et al., 2009). These three approaches inspire an approach to HCI that we call Adaptive Interaction.

The framework also relates very closely, and in a particular way, to more general work on the role of optimality analysis in cognitive science, which, especially with respect to Bayesian analysis, has seen a huge surge of interest in Cognitive Science, beginning with the work of Anderson (1990). The work of Gray and colleagues on "Soft Constraints hypothesis" is particularly close to our approach, both theoretically and empirically (Gray & Fu, 2004; Gray et al., 2006).

Finally, the framework certainly has close relations within the HCI and Human Factors literatures (Norman, 1983; Young & MacLean, 1988; Dessouky et al., 1995; Baron & Kleinman, 1969) - especially, although not limited to, Information Foraging Theory, inasmuch as it borrows the theoretical framework of Optimal Foraging Theory (Pirolli & Card, 1999), and much of the work on Fitts's Law (although rarely are the framework issues which we stress articulated in this work, they are implicit in some of the analyses). Also, there is our own earlier plea for decision-theoretic analysis of certain HCI phenomena, which we revisit in this lecture (S. J. Payne et al., 2001). The framework is also influenced by ideas in Machine Learning, including (Russell & Subramanian, 1995; Sutton & Barto, 1998), but these are not explored further here.

We begin by specifying the framework, exposing its roots in the writings cited above. We then argue, in general terms, why we believe such a theoretically oriented framework may have practical implications for HCI. Following these general arguments we review some example issues which illustrate instantiations of the framework and its applications to HCI design issues: some of these are classical approaches in the literature (e.g., using Signal Detection Theory (Swets et al., 1961) to measure and support diagnostic decision making; deciding whether to trust a vendor); others are our own ongoing research projects (e.g., accessing on-line reviews to inform purchasing decisions; skim-reading to allocate limited attention across an over-abundance of relevant text).

Because Information Foraging is already widely known by HCI researchers, and because it is widely regarded as a successful example of theory-led HCI, we will begin by exposing and describing the key framing assumptions of Optimal Foraging Theory—the biological enterprise from which Information Foraging drew its main inspiration (Pirolli & Card, 1999). Our aim is to show how these assumptions have much in common with other approaches to human behaviour, and that this shared framework has a much broader applicability to Human-Computer Interaction than in understanding information foraging (although that is indeed a key contribution, and one on which we hope to build).

According to Stephens & Krebs (1986), optimality models comprise three types of assumption:

1. Decision assumptions that focus on particular problems or choices - isolating these from the complex of animal behaviour;

2. Currency assumptions which specify how alternatives are to be evaluated;

3. Constraint assumptions that express limits on the animal's feasible choices.

These assumptions map straightforwardly onto the terminology of Adaptive Interaction (Figure 1.1). The decision assumptions are assumptions concerning the ecology of interaction. The currency assumptions concern utility functions, and the constraints concern the cognitive mechanisms.

To exemplify these assumptions, let us briefly consider the most famous result in Optimal Foraging Theory, namely Charnov's Marginal Value Theorem (Charnov, 1976), also described by Stephens & Krebs (1986) and Pirolli & Card (1999).

The decision that Charnov analysed is the decision of when to quit a food patch. Consider, for example, a bird foraging for berries in an orchard of fruit trees. When the bird alights on a tree, it begins to eat berries. How long should it remain in the same patch—the same tree—eating berries before it accepts the energy cost of flying to a nearby tree? The currency assumed by the model is rate of gain of energy. If berries remained equally easy to obtain until the tree was empty, the obvious solution—the one yielding optimal rate of energy gain—would be to remain in the tree until it is exhausted. But what if the berries become gradually harder and harder to find or reach (as intuition suggests they would). Charnov (1976) proved that the bird can optimise their overall rate of energy gain by staying in the tree until the current marginal rate of gain of energy (or berries) is equal to the average rate across the whole foraging episode so far (say, time in the orchard).

One of the three types of assumption is not mentioned in the above description, that of constraint. Indeed, Charnov's theorem does not assume any constraint—rather it computes the optimum strategy for some ideal agent (which may well be unrealistic—can a bird track average and marginal rates of gain?!). For all its success and influence, then, Charnov's theorem is rather idealised compared with optimal foraging theories in general. Nevertheless, it has proved useful in explaining animal behaviour and in computing what the optimum behaviour is for comparison against empirical data.

Although not explicit in the narrative above, one might regard the bird's problem as to choose a single strategy from a strategy space, defined by the range between leaving immediately—immediately after a single berry has been consumed—or leaving only after all the berries in a tree have been consumed. Stephens & Krebs (1986) prefer to avoid the term strategy, believing it to be stripped of much meaning through over use, but we will use it in exactly this sense.

Strategy and strategy space are key terms in the next expression of the framework we wish to describe, which is due to Erev, Gopher, Roth and colleagues (Erev & Roth, 1998; Roth & Erev,

1995; Erev & Gopher, 1999), and is called Cognitive Game Theory. Our impression is that this work, although in the neighbouring field of human factors engineering, is hardly known in HCI and much less well-known in cognitive science than it deserves to be.

Erev & Gopher (1999) motivate their approach with a distinction that, it seems to us, has been very important in the use of various theoretical and methodological approaches to HCI, namely the difference between two questions concerning user behaviour: what *can* the user do versus what will the user *try* to do. Erev & Gopher (1999) characterise cognitive psychology as focussing on the former question, whereas "social psychology and microeconomic research" focus on the latter question. They suggest that applied research needs to address both questions, because real behaviour emerges from an interaction between cognitive constraints and incentives (which expressed in some currency provide a means for specifying how alternatives are evaluated).

Cognitive Game Theory begins by characterising classical Game Theory in terms of the three components that are required to predict performance on a game: the set of available strategies (Erev & Gopher (1999) define a strategy as an ensemble of acts triggered by specific pre-conditions); an incentive structure; and a decision-rule for choosing which strategy will be selected.

Cognitive Game Theory allows two complications to this scheme. The set of available strategies is affected by constraints imposed by the human information processing system. Only those strategies which the user is cognitively equipped to perform are considered. The decision-rule for choosing among strategies (which is traditionally assumed to be currency maximisation) is replaced with an assumption of adaptive learning. Cognitive Game Theory proposes that a reinforcement learning mechanism assigns values to strategies on the basis of experience.

If we compare these three components to the framework assumptions of optimal foraging theory, the difference is one of emphasis. Stephens & Krebs (1986) highlight the importance of constraints, whereas for Cognitive Game Theory these are assumed to delimit the space of possible strategies. Cognitive Game Theory highlights the idea of adaptive learning of strategies whereas Optimal Foraging Theory is more usually concerned with behaviours that are fully learned or that are acquired through evolution, and so assumes the simple rule of "maximise." An application of Cognitive Game Theory to team signal detection tasks is reviewed in Section 3.

Finally, we turn to the work by Howes et al. (2009) on Cognitively Bounded Rational Analysis (CBRA). The idea that people are able to learn to select utility maximizing strategies again plays an important role as does the idea that the available strategies are constrained by the organism (Howes et al., 2004). In addition, this work explores theories of the constraints that are encoded as computational cognitive architectures. Theories of the cognitive architecture include ACT-R (Anderson et al., 2004), EPIC (Meyer & Kieras, 1997), and Soar (Newell, 1990). They have played a continuing role in developing HCI theory since the foundation of the field (Card et al., 1983). They can be seen as more psychologically plausible theories of interaction than are provided by approximate notations such as GOMS or KLM, though they share some assumptions in common.

Howes et al.'s (2009) primary concern was to offer a framework that could help realize the potential of cognitive architectures for predicting, as opposed to merely describing, interactive behaviour. In many ways, the goal of prediction is at the heart of the idea that behavioral science can inform the interaction-design process. One problem addressed by Howes et al. was that the extreme flexibility of theories of psychological information processing means that any given interactive task may be approached via an unbounded variety of strategies, making it very hard to discern which strategy the architecture predicts. While it must be the case that a theory of human cognition is able to flexibly select between many strategies, it does not seem right that the theory makes little commitment as to which strategies will be preferred. Howes et al. addressed this problem by assuming that people select strategies so as to maximize an instructed utility function.

This framework is in a sense the common ground between Optimal Foraging Theory and Cognitive Game Theory: the force of Howes et al's contribution was to combine analysis of the constraints imposed by the human cognitive architecture with an analysis of utility functions (the currency the agent is assumed to care about, and how payoff in this currency varies as a function of the various performance parameters, such as speed and accuracy). Through this combination it is possible to make quantitative predictions of behaviour in interactive tasks—by exploring the range of possible strategies allowed by the architecture, and predicting that strategies will be chosen so as to maximise utility. This approach avoids the problems associated with choosing a single plausible strategy, programming the architecture with this strategy, and fitting quantitative free parameters to the data.

The work conducted by Howes et al. was part of a programme of work motivated by HCI design problems in complex dynamic task environments such as typing (M. R. Smith et al., 2008), the flight deck (Howes et al., 2004; Lewis et al., 2004; Eng et al., 2006; Tollinger et al., 2005; Duggan et al., 2004; Vera et al., 2004; Waldron et al., 2008; Howes et al., 2005), and driving (Brumby et al., 2009, 2007; Janssen et al., 2011), as well as information intensive decision problems including product choice (Lelis & Howes, 2008, 2011). The adaptation of strategies to constraints is a pervasive aspect of these high pressure environments. One of the primary goals of this work has been to make developments in cognitive science available to HCI and vice-versa.

We can see then that all three of these approaches (OFT, CGT, and CBRA) share a basic commitment to the three components that were made first in OFT. These involve assumptions concerning: decision problems, a currency (expressing a utility function), and constraints. In fact, it is worth explicitly mapping these components to HCI:

1. Decision assumptions focus on particular problems or choices—isolating these from the complex of human interactive behaviour. Historically HCI has naturally cleaved into reasonably well-defined decision problems: Where to look for information, how to manage email, whether to adopt Twitter or Facebook or both. However, while such issues have been observed (Whittaker et al., 2006) the decision assumptions have rarely been addressed as an explicit scientific problem. Explicitly doing so may be fruitful.

2. Currency assumptions specify how alternatives are to be evaluated. In HCI, currency has typically been defined in terms of speed and accuracy. More recent efforts have also been made to extend currency assumptions to more experiential factors such as calmness, happiness, etc.

The utilities operating in a given situation are one way in which "context" influences behaviour and elucidating this is a key challenge that our framework clarifies.

3. Constraint assumptions express limits on the user's feasible choices. Ultimately in HCI design the constraints that are malleable and that are the focus of the discipline are those that are imposed by the design (the task environment). However, behaviour is sometimes more constrained by cognition than by the design, so that the potential of a design cannot be exploited by humans. Cognitive constraints therefore provides a critical limiting factor on design.

While emphasis varies, these three components imply a space of strategies from which a predicted strategy can be derived through utility maximisation (Howes et al., 2009) or utility learning (Erev & Gopher, 1999). Importantly, the explicit computational representation of constraints on the one hand and strategies and utility on the other precisely defines the relationship between what people can do and what they choose to do which is critical to a scientific basis for understanding HCI. When applied to HCI tasks the three components amount to the assumption that people can be understood as maximally adaptive given cognitive and experiential constraints. We refer to this view as the Adaptive Interaction framework.

Despite its scientific pedigree, we recognise that, for many HCI researchers, the Adaptive Interaction framework may seem unpromising. The relative simplicity of the tasks addressed by OFT, CGT and CBRA, the wealth of quantitative data that must be explained, and despite all this, the exacting theoretical niceties that must be broached to approach a computational explanation of the major phenomena all stand in stark contrast to the typical situation in HCI, where scientists and designers may have to understand important limits on the performance of complex tasks which have seen relatively little empirical investigation. Worse, perhaps, it is widely assumed in the behavioral sciences, not just HCI, that people are not optimal (Chase et al., 1998; Fu & Gray, 2006). These claims come in many forms but include: the brain is a kludge (Marcus, 2009), irrational biases are an empirical fact (Ariely, 2009; Bowers & Davis, 2012), and that optimisation is computationally intractable (Chase et al., 1998). So why do we believe that the Adaptive Interaction framework, inspired by frameworks designed to make precise quantitative predictions concerning performance on simple tasks, will be relevant to HCI?

The answer is multi-layered. Through a series of examples, in this lecture we seek to demonstrate that:

1. By providing the means to understand strategies, and how they are adapted with experience to the affordances and constraints provided by particular designs, the framework offers a means for HCI theory to break into the task-artifact cycle, which has important implications for design evaluation and comparison.

2. The framework is as relevant to social phenomena (and therefore current HCI challenges), including economic relationships, community relationships, and friendship, as it is to simple perceptual-motor tasks or foraging tasks. For example: reputation games, ultimatum games, etc.

3. The framework has potential heuristic benefits and is not wedded to its computational analysis.

4. The framework is not in fact disproved by evidence for apparent suboptimality and bias. In fact, this evidence is often over-stated and is widely misinterpreted. It can only be interpreted safely, we argue, as evidence of theory failure, not as evidence of suboptimality. This is a difficult issue that we will return to in the Discussion, see Section 11.

In supporting these claims we will see that one key emphasis for us will be in a focus on the strategy space. The advantage of thinking in terms of a *strategy space* is that it allows investigators to understand human behaviour relative to alternatives. Instead of being content, as ethnographic investigations must remain, with describing what people do, the approach encourages a comparison of such empirically observed strategies against the other possible strategies in the space. In this sense, though it may seem counterintuitive to express it in this way, our framework is related to Design Rationale (MacLean et al., 1991). Design Rationale gains traction by exposing the design space in which a point design is situated, and why the point design is the way it is, compared with neighbouring alternatives. We propose exactly this kind of argument concerning strategies. Indeed, because strategies and design choices are so intimately connected, because HCI design choices will afford and constrain available strategies (shaping the environmental constraints that are experienced by users and that are one of the foundations of the framework), our strategy analyses may be considered a kind of design rationale.

The assumption of optimality suggests that any observed strategy can be understood as being better than alternatives—once the utility function has been specified to allow such comparison—or if alternatives appear to better but not used, to provoke an exploration for why this might be. Because of the optimality assumption the investigator can look for poorly specified utilities, or constraints not yet identified, or opportunities to learn not yet realised.

In the remainder of this lecture we exercise and illustrate this general framework by reviewing empirical work on specific HCI questions. Because Erev & Gopher (1999) and Howes et al. (2009) both present their frameworks as generalizations of the approach taken by Signal Detection Theory, and because SDT is the best developed example of the approach with arguably the most developed mathematical analysis and certainly the widest range of applications to real design problems we will begin there. However, because SDT is widely known and reviewed impressively in many places (Swets et al., 1961; D. M. Green & Swets, 1966) we will make our overview brief, and focussed on the way that SDT illustrates the more general framework. We will try to argue how SDT models can be extended to address collaborative diagnosis by human-machine systems, which is very much an open research question which exposes important issues for CSCW more generally.

CHAPTER 3

Signal Detection Theory and Collaborative Diagnosis

3.1 BASIC SIGNAL DETECTION

Many important decisions including those supported by technology are binary diagnostic decisions. Many of these decisions are binary diagnostic decisions, in which evidence for the presence of a condition must be assessed. Such diagnosis is common in the clinical domain: does this patient have dementia according to the cognitive-behavioural evidence? Does this lung have a tumor according to the X-ray? And also in all kinds of safety-related engineering tasks: Is this jet-engine cracked? As well as in many of the document processing tasks that have been studied in HCI, sometimes under the banner of information foraging: Is this paper relevant to my current project?

Aspects of how diagnostic decisions are made and can be measured are common across all such domains, because in every task the decision is made under uncertainty, depending on interpreting noisy evidence for the presence of a signal, and in using some criterion to determine when the evidence is sufficient. The most widespread mathematical model of this process is Signal Detection Theory (SDT), which in its simplest form presumes that the evidence can be modelled in terms of variation along a single quantitative dimension, with the criterion defined as a value on this dimension. Technology design may reduce noise, making the decision easier, or it may increase noise, making it harder, but it will not eliminate the importance of a decision threshold which is vital for understanding behaviour and design.

Figure 3.1 shows the classic depiction of this situation: in this idealised graph the distributions of both signal and noise with respect to the evidence dimension are roughly normal, and they overlap so that the diagnosis is necessarily error-prone. In general, there are two components to the variance (noise) in both signal and noise distributions external or environmental noise and internal noise in the percept. In experimental investigations of SDT, investigators can manipulate the former, but not the latter. Similarly, designers of information technology can change the external noise with new, hopefully noise reducing, interfaces but cannot control the internal noise generated in the percept.

It can be seen that reducing the spread of the signal and the noise distributions or increasing their separation, perhaps through improved interface design, will allow the observer to select a criterion that returns a greater ratio of hits to false alarms. In the extreme the two distributions do not overlap and the criterion entirely separates hits and false alarms. A measure of the degree of overlap of the distributions is d'.

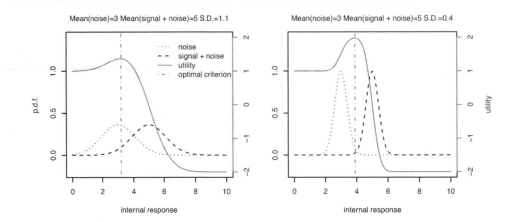

Figure 3.1: Two panels each representing Signal Detection Theory (SDT). In both, the evidence for a diagnosis is represented on the x-axis and the probability density function (pdf) on the y-axis. In the left panel there is more noise than in the right panel. The noise is represented by the spread of the noise and of the 'signal + noise' distributions. The increased noise in the left panel is evident in that the spread of the distributions covers six units of internal response on the x-axis whereas the spread of the distributions in the right panel covers only two units (e.g., from 2 to 4). In the right panel, the variance in the noise and signal has been reduced, perhaps with some new interface design. The new design increases the discrimination between the two distributions and as a consequence, if the user selects a new criterion, a higher payoff can be achieved.

$$d' = \frac{separation}{spread}$$

It can also be seen by inspecting Figure 3.1 that a shift of the criterion, that is a shift of strategy, will change the proportion of the four outcome types that SDT distinguishes: hits (where the signal is present and judged to be present), misses (where the signal is present but judged absent), correct rejections (where the signal is absent and judged absent), and false alarms (signal absent but judged present).

Because decision behaviour represents a trade-off under the control of the decision threshold, the standard measures of diagnosis of performance rely on the Receiver Operating Characteristic Curve (ROC). The standard measures of diagnosis performance rely on the ROC curve, which plots the conditional probability of hits (P yes|signal) on the Y-axis against the conditional probability of false alarms (P yes|no-signal) on the X-axis. ROC curves show how hits and false alarms can be traded off at a given level of discrimination (see Figure 3.2). More importantly, they show how designs can be compared. Better interfaces are associated with higher values of d'.

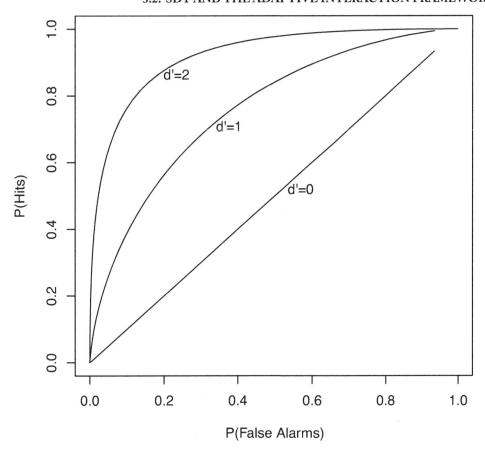

Figure 3.2: A typical set of Receiver Operating Characteristic Curves (ROC) for increasing values of the discrimination index d'. The less the spread of the signal and noise distributions and the greater the gap between their means then the greater the value of d'. Higher values of d' are associated with better interface designs.

3.2   SDT AND THE ADAPTIVE INTERACTION FRAMEWORK

In terms of the framework, the strategy space that an agent considers is given by the range of the criterion parameter, whereas the environmental and cognitive constraints combine to fix the agent's sensitivity.

There are many applications of SDT that show how analysis of the optimum criterion has important implications for the design of diagnostic technologies and protocols. In binary diagnosis tasks, overall utility of decisions depends on the utility of the four possible outcomes: hit, miss, false alarm, correct rejection. Thus, the criterion must be set by considering these, together with the base-rate for signals (because likelihood of signal given evidence is a matter of likelihood updating, as given by Bayes theorem).

3.3   ADAPTATION

Signal Detection Theory is exemplary in showing that even a simple task can be analysed in terms of architectural/environmental constraints and a discretionary or decision-making layer, in which one strategy is chosen from the strategy space. It allows the optimality assumption to be, in principle, straightforwardly tested given an agent's ability to discriminate signal from noise, and imposing a particular set of payoffs for hits, false alarms, misses, and correct rejections. Can the agent discover the optimal criterion?

In fact, the evidence concerning whether people find optimal criteria is somewhat mixed, or at least has led to different conclusions. Most investigations of SDT, as noted above, use perceptual discrimination tasks, for which variance in signal and noise will come from both environmental and perceptual noise. But SDT is by no means limited to perceptual discrimination tasks, and some of the most impressive tests of the optimality assumption sidestep the problem of perceptual noise by giving participants direct access to a quantitative value on the evidence scale. For example, Kubovy et al. (1971) presented participants with four-digit numbers, each drawn from one of two normal distributions with equal standard deviations, and means one s.d. apart. Participants were told that the distributions represented the heights of women and men, that women and men had an equal chance of being sampled on each trial, and that their task was to decide on each trial whether the height was that of a man or a woman. Five different payoff conditions were used, varying from the simple case in which correct responses received 1 point to a skewed payoff function in which correct responses to one category received 9 points, whereas correct responses to the other received 1 point. Errors were uniformly rewarded 0 points.

For such utility functions and base rates it is simple to compute the optimal criterion, but not so simple for the experimental participant, who simply makes a response and receives some payoff note that for a participant the very same response to the same stimulus can receive different payoffs on different trials because of the essential uncertainty of the task. Nevertheless Kubovy et al. (1971) report that after a considerable number of trials (2000) participants' behaviour was best modelled by assuming a static, optimal criterion has been set. Subsequent work has used less practice to expose the difficulties participants face learning towards these optima (exposing the so-called 'sluggish beta' phenomenon, in which criterion is shifted less than it should in response to payoff asymmetries), but such limits may be explained by the limits on experience, and the constraints on learning, rather than threatening the optimality assumption per se. Indeed, Erev & Gopher (1999) and colleagues have shown that a simple reinforcement learning algorithm can explain participants' thresholds.

In an applied domain, Chi & Drury (1998) studied circuit inspection tasks using model stimuli very like those of Kubovy et al. (1971), and found that the optimal threshold shift computed from SDT is a better fit to participants' decisions than simpler models that take into account only the base rate or only the payoffs. They argue that the model has distinct applied benefits in allowing a prediction of human performance for function allocation against machine inspection. This use of SDT to extrapolate human performance from measured points to more general task parameters, so as to allow generalisation from necessarily limited empirical investigations, is an important applied use of decision-theoretic models that is echoed in HCI work on Fitts's Law (see Section 5).

One way in which SDT theory can be applied is in support of empirical evaluation of different diagnostic instruments (for example, cognitive tests for the early signs of dementia). Even the simple analysis above makes clear that it will not generally be sufficient to evaluate such a test by setting a single criterion score and measuring the accuracy of diagnoses.

A better evaluative procedure would be to vary the criterion and plot the ROC curve, so that the overall accuracy of the test could be computed, and so that the criterion could be adjusted in a way that is sensitive to the base rates and to the relative costs of the two kinds of error. Such evaluative data is indeed reported in some research on diagnostic tests, but, at least in the case of HCI, it is by no means widespread. Too often, it appears to the authors, it is the case that HCI studies report hits but not false alarms, for example.

In many complex real-world diagnostic procedures a single diagnostic test is likely to be only one piece of evidence among many. This raises the very important question about how individual sources of evidence—each with their own discrimination accuracy and ROC curve—should be combined. We return to this issue below.

3.4 COLLABORATIVE DIAGNOSIS

Although much research on SDT has focussed on understanding the performance of individuals engaged in diagnosis tasks, the theory can be extended to collaborative diagnosis, for which it leads to some very interesting and applicable results and research questions. We contend that this theory has considerable potential for new insights for the design of collaborative technologies.

Perhaps the most general question that can be asked—although mathematically quite complex—is how to derive optimal performance from a team of observers who have varying discrimination capabilities and access to only partially overlapping evidence of varying diagnostic value.

Pete et al. (1993) considered teams organised hierarchically, in which a single decision maker is charged with receiving and combining all subordinates' decisions. Optimal performance by such a team will depend on each individual having access to all team members' ability to discriminate and response criteria, so that they may mutually constrain each other's criteria. Or, to put it another way, given that discrimination capabilities are fixed, the strategic optimum for the group will depend on the individuals setting their criteria collaboratively. Not surprisingly, perhaps Pete et al discovered that teams of three found such an optimum impossible to achieve: it is hard to imagine how an individual team member might learn the effects of his or her own criterion on group performance when this depends on the shifting criteria of his or her teammates.

Nevertheless, team members can sometimes learn to adjust their criteria according to game-like utility functions, as shown in a set of studies by Erev & Gopher (1999), reviewed in the chapter from which their "Cognitive Game Theory" manifesto note above is taken (Erev & Gopher,

1999). Erev & Gopher (1999) asked pairs of participants to make independent diagnostic decisions, but presented them with utilities that depended not only on their own responses relative to the truth of the signal, but also on each others' responses in a variety of games. For example, in a 'Consensus Game' participants were rewarded if they both made a correct diagnostic decision, but punished otherwise. Participants were not allowed to collaborate—as in the classic Prisoner's Dilemma they had to make a response without knowing their partner's response.

Erev & Gopher (1999) report that participants gradually adjust their decision thresholds according to these interdependent utility functions, and that the incremental improvement of their thresholds with experience and feedback is well-modelled by a simple reinforcement learning algorithm.

A much more straightforward model of group SDT is to allow each judge to make an independent decision and to determine the team decision by a majority vote. Such a scheme is a simple and effective way of increasing the accuracy of diagnostic decisions, as shown by Sorkin et al. (1998). These authors analysed the predicted performance of odd-numbered groups of decision makers using majority voting schemes. The analysis shows that diagnostic accuracy is optimal for the bare majority scheme and gets progressively less accurate as well as more conservative as the votes required for a signal judgment increase towards unanimity. Also see Sorkin et al. (2001); Sorkin & Dai (1994); Sorkin et al. (1988).

One further simple model for organizing joint Signal Detection is to utilise the judgments of different agents in series. This is a common arrangement when automated alarms are used in conjunction with human operators, as in aircraft or power plants. In such situations the human operator performs what Sorkin & Woods (1985), in a paper in the very first issue of the journal Human-Computer Interaction, call an "alerted monitor" role. For a simple example, consider a domestic smoke alarm. The alarm acts as an alert to a human monitor (the home owner), who then considers other evidence to diagnose the situation and act accordingly.

The performance of the automated alarm can itself be considered in terms of Signal Detection Theory, with the alarm triggering whenever evidence (whether from a single source or integrated over several sources) exceeds a pre-determined threshold. Adjusting this threshold, as the design engineer must do, will, of course, change the relative frequency of hits, misses, and false positives. A common practice is, apparently, to set the automated alarm thresholds so as to optimise the automated alarm's performance (in terms of the relative utilities of hits and false alarms). However, such a setting may not optimize the performance of the overall human-machine system, because the human operator is likely to adapt their own strategy according to the automated system's behaviour.

As in the case of the smoke alarm, the evidence interpreted by the automatic and human components of the system is likely to be different, at least to some extent, and the human's response to the alarm is likely to depend on assumptions about the automatic response criterion (in particular false alarm rate) as well as the importance of the condition being signaled. Sorkin and Woods analyse a number of potential dependencies between the human operator's and the automated system's independent response criteria.

One plausible case is that the human will become more conservative as the automatic alarm becomes more liberal. A further and more damaging case is that a busy human operator may allocate less attention to monitoring an alarm state if the automatic system is too liberal. In such cases, the human operator's discrimination capability (as well as response criterion) is affected by the automatic system's response criterion.

Sorkin & Woods (1985) show how to analyse such systems as two stage signal detection, with a human-machine system ROC curve resulting from the serial performance of the two stages (machine then human). Such serial systems may also, of course, apply in some human-human collaborations. For example, longlist-shortlist judgment systems (e.g., in employment interviews) are typically of this kind. It seems plausible, given the above analysis, that the participants in such systems will need careful training if they are to adjust their own thresholds so as to optimize the overall system performance.

An interesting recent study of collaborative signal detection used a classical perceptual discrimination task to ask how pairs of detectors would spontaneously collaborate on a decision (Bahrami et al., 2010). By using a forced choice task, in which either the first or second stimulus of every pair contained a signal (with signal strength varying), this study ignored the threshold-decision layer of general SDT tasks, but nevertheless speaks to our concerns.

Bahrami et al. (2010) identified four a priori models by which pairs of detectors might combine their judgements, in the case where they disagree, and compared the performance of each model with that of the better performing individual in the pair. First, they may toss a coin. It is clear that this model will not perform as well as the better individual in the pair, because it will commit half the additional errors of the weaker member. Second, the pair may learn, if given feedback, who is the more discriminating member and use that member's response. Obviously, this model will (eventually) perform just as well as the more discriminating member. Third, the judgements may be weighed by confidence (an individual's estimate of the likelihood that their judgment is correct). This model will perform better than the more discriminating member, provided the two members are fairly close in their discrimination capability. If the two members vary greatly in discrimination, the confidence-weighed judgment may be worse than the more discriminating member's. Finally, the Direct Signal Sharing model assumed that the two participants could share the mean and standard deviation (or confidence interval) of each percept. This model would do at least as well as the best member, whatever the discrepancy of the members' discrimination capabilities. By manipulating environmental noise separately for each individual, these models were tested. The participants agreed/joint responses were well predicted by the confidence model.

The models briefly noted above, and the empirical finding, have direct practical implications, as sketched below. But also, the finding that pair performance was sometimes weaker than Direct Signal Sharing predicted may seem to challenge the optimality assumption. DSS has been used as a successful model of individuals' multi-modal signal detection, when evidence from a different sensory modality must be combined, so there is evidence that people do perceive means and confidence intervals of perceptual signals (contrast differences is the case in point). The most likely explanation is that the pairs could not find any way of communicating the signal means and confidence intervals to each other. Confidence, on the other hand, is relatively easy to share, at least coarsely.

This analysis illustrates that when analysing team performance the constraints of mechanism and environment (Figure 1.1) will include constraints on collaboration such as communication bandwidth.

In combination these studies suggest important avenues for practical research and potential progress in the many real-world diagnostic situations where teams, supported by technology, must agree on diagnostic decisions, as is true in many medical settings, as well as many commonplace organizational decisions (such as personnel selection).

To optimize the overall performance of such collaborative systems, it is essential to consider the interrelations of each individual's (and each instrument's) discrimination and response bias. This is perhaps the fundamental insight of all the above studies, and we believe it has important and little recognised implications. For example, if a new medical test is to be employed, then it is crucial that the response threshold is chosen not so as to optimize the diagnosis provided by the test, but rather to optimize the diagnoses of the diagnostic system to which the test contributes (very often a part serial part parallel system in which the test result acts as an alert to a later stage of the process).

A further very general issue in the design of collaborative diagnostic worksystems is the issue of noise in evidence (the essential assumption of the SDT paradigm, see Figure 3.1). The benefit of combining multiple detectors is greater when the correlation of the noise in their judgments is minimised.

This is, in fact, a general issue in "Wisdom of Crowds" effects, well made by the first and most famous such phenomenon. When Galton (1907) examined the voting cards after visitors to a fair had entered a competition to guess the weight of an ox, he discovered that the median of their responses produced a remarkably accurate estimate (to within 1% of the true weight), much more accurate than that of single expert judges. This is initially counterintuitive, but arises for elementary reasons: each judge's guess can be considered a combination of truth and noise. The "truth" is determined by their experience of weights and densities in the world, their visual percept of the ox, etc. The noise may have any number of sources, but, crucially, will vary randomly from person to person, and so will average to zero.

This logic would only be threatened if the observers' noise was correlated. Ironically, such correlation may be fostered by discussion: imagine if all the visitors of the fair had engaged in discussion with one another before reporting their best guesses. The famous Asch paradigm (Asch, 1951) has shown the extent to which individual judgments can be biased by social influence, and Lorenz et al. (2011) showed that exposing people to others' judgments undermines the wisdom of crowds effect in estimation tasks.

This line of argument points to the dangers of discussion in collaborative diagnostic situations, and yet, to our limited knowledge such discussion is commonplace in medical settings, where multi-disciplinary teams are often engaged in diagnosis decisions. We are not in a position to argue that this is inappropriate, but the question is definitely worth asking. Perhaps discussion has some other justification, such as training less expert members by exposure to more expert members' reasoning. Or perhaps the value of discussion could be increased by designing, and technologically supporting, collaboration protocols which try to insure the independence of noise, and which are sensitive to the findings reviewed above concerning the communication of confidence in initially independent judgments and the way team members may adjust decision thresholds in the light of their collaborators' behaviour.

CHAPTER 4

Discretionary Task Interleaving

Multitasking is an everyday reality for many people. The management of time across multiple activities is a crucial skill that many researchers in HCI have attempted to understand, so as to inform the design of technological support. In this section we will review some of this HCI research on multitasking, focussing on our own theoretical contribution (especially S. J. Payne et al., 2007) and its relation to the Adaptive Interaction framework, as well as some later work which addresses related issues. This work, on "Discretionary task interleaving" is closely related to the work on skim reading, reviewed below, in that it uses our general framework, and aspects of foraging theory in particular to explore the utility space of decisions concerning what to work on when, and the strategies that multitaskers may use to maximize utility by switching among tasks.

In an observational study of information workers, González & Mark (2005) reported that workers switched activities very frequently, indeed on average about every three minutes. Many of these switches were necessitated by external interruptions such as phone calls or visits, but a large number, as many as half of the switches, were due to "self interruption" or discretionary switching. Further studies have confirmed the tendency to manage multitasking by choosing to switch tasks frequently (e.g., Mark et al., 2005; Arora et al., 2011).

From an Adaptive Interaction perspective, we assume that discretionary switching between tasks is achieved with strategies, sensitive to the particular ecology, that allow workers to optimise their utility, see Figure 1.1. Sometimes, it is not immediately clear why this should be so. If an information worker has two articles to write (we suspect that many readers will recognise this situation!), why might it be optimal to interrupt the writing of one so as to work on the other, later to return to the first? We suppose (see S. J. Payne et al., 2007), that time spent on each of the two articles results in utility for the worker, but that the function of this gain curve is, in each case, initially unknown to the writer, and can only be estimated and projected by working on each task. Let us assume that the problem the writer must solve is to distribute time across the articles so as to maximize overall gain (and perhaps as well, given intrinsic uncertainty about the amount of total time available for the two tasks, to maximize this overall gain incrementally, over increasing time windows). The only way to accomplish this is to track the shifting gain functions on each of the two tasks, thus necessitating switching frequently between the two, relative to the total notional available time for each.

This informal analysis suggests some important issues for the understanding of multitasking (or more accurately, it shows how the main constructs of the Adaptive Interaction framework are relevant to this domain). First, it confirms that the key concept of utility can be applied to throw light on multitasking strategies, but beyond this, it shows how the shape of the utility gain curve over time is a very important characteristic of a task or activity (S. J. Payne et al., 2007), and that an important problem for the worker is, in some sense, to track, model, and project this gain curve.

The utility gain curves of different tasks vary not only in coarse shape, but also in character. Some tasks, such as the article-writing example, may have a gain curve which is initially nearly linear, but which, as the article becomes complete, is subject to diminishing returns. Diminishing returns gain curves are a standard assumption in many foraging tasks, and characterise the tasks studied by S. J. Payne et al. (2007) which are reviewed below. Other tasks that have been studied as multitasking, such as steering a vehicle, concern a dynamic environment which the operator must monitor, so that the relation of "gain" to time on task is radically non-linear, the temporal function is perhaps better viewed as avoidance of loss, rather than gain, and what is required is regular intervention rather than prolonged activity (Brumby et al., 2009; Janssen et al., 2011; Farmer et al., 2011). Still other tasks, such as those most often considered in scheduling theory (Dessouky et al., 1995) may be considered to have utility only on completion, which is assumed to take a certain amount of time.

4.1   MECHANISM CONSTRAINTS

As well as utility and the need to monitor gain curves, strategies for allocating time across multiple tasks must reflect cognitive constraints on task performance. These are the mechanisms in Figure 1.1. Particularly relevant in this context are constraints on task switching.

A burgeoning literature in experimental psychology on task switching exposes and analyses such cognitive-architectural constraints on the ability to switch from one "task set" to another. In this paradigm, a typical experiment would require participants to respond to the same stimulus in one of two ways depending on the current "task set." If the stimulus was a digit, one task set could be to respond "even" or "odd," the second task set to respond "less than five" or "greater than five." The task set might be imposed by instruction and therefore need to be kept in mind, or signaled perceptually, or both. For example, in the "alternating runs" paradigm (R. D. Rogers & Monsell, 1995), participants perform one task for two trials, and then the second task for the next two trials and so on.

The fundamental finding from such experiments is that there exists a "switch cost": The first task of a new task set is performed more slowly than subsequent ones. Experimental explorations have focussed on what factors moderate this switch cost. Beginning with (Allport et al., 1994), much literature has reported the effects of manipulations of the relative difficulty of the tasks, the response-stimulus intervals (RSIs) between tasks, the compatibility of the responses and so on. Theoretical interest has focussed on the cognitive constraints that lead to costs, and the extent to which switch cost reflects the operation of a unified central executive, as proposed in the Baddeley/Hitch model of working memory (Baddeley & Hitch, 1974). In other words, in keeping with our introductory remarks about cognitive psychology, interest has focussed on trying to uncover cognitive architectural constraints on what people can and cannot do.

A broader theory of these constraints has been put forward by Salvucci & Taatgen (2008). As noted by these authors, multitasking may be considered according to a temporal continuum, with dual task performance at one end and more extended switching between tasks at the other. Many theoretical treatments of classic "dual task" paradigm (Styles, 2006) performance, consider it to be a matter of switching and time-sharing across tasks, with mental resources being allocated to one or another task in turn. Salvucci and Taatgen extend this tradition by collapsing over the temporal dimension in terms of a theory of cognitive constraints that apply independently of the variation in timescale: in particular, the various memory loads of managing multiple goals, rehearsing multiple problem states and so on (see also Altmann & Trafton (2002)). Their work focusses on the cognitive costs and benefits of goal rehearsal strategies, and the relation to our primary interest in the decision-theoretic layer, the multitaskers choice of strategy, is that these constraints must influence the parametric properties of the multitasker's choice of time-distribution strategy as well as the precise effectiveness of switching.

4.2   SOLVING THE ADAPTIVE PROBLEM

To summarise, so far, we have argued for two important factors in switching between tasks as a basic strategy for managing multiple tasks. First, there is the informational advantage of switching: switching allows the multitasker to experience and track the gain curves of the tasks that must be completed, which is surely necessary if time is to be allocated across tasks so as to maximize overall utility. Second there is a set of cognitive constraints which is likely to make switching, to some extent, inefficient because demanding of extraneous cognitive processing (although for other tasks, there is the possibility that time away from a task will have a positive effect in itself, as addressed by the controversial literature on "incubation effects" in problem solving (see S. M. Smith & Blankenship (1991)).

Multitaskers must somehow manage the problem of time allocation according to the various utilities of tasks, while being sensitive to the effects of their own cognitive constraints.

A thorough discussion of such issues, as well as some interesting empirical work was offered by Neville Moray and colleagues in the 1990s, through a comparison between scheduling theory (a well-developed branch of engineering) and human strategic control (Moray et al., 1991; Dessouky et al., 1995). Analysis of scheduling considers various aspects of the utility of task completion, such as the importance of deadlines and lateness or "tardiness" as well as aspects of task dependencies, etc. The scheduling rules considered in most depth by Moray and colleagues assume that tasks have fixed durations and deadlines and utilities that depend on their relative priority, with penalties if the deadline or due date is missed. The efficacy of rules such as "Earliest due date first" and "Shortest processing time first" can be analysed according to the properties of the set of tasks that need to be scheduled. In Moray et al's laboratory paradigm, participants scheduled their activity across a set of tasks with varying durations-to-completion and varying deadlines or due dates. Moray reported that many participants approached optimal scheduling performance, although some showed marked departures. When time constraints were more severe, performance was worse, because time to consider and plan a good strategy was in direct competition with time to work on the primary tasks. This finding is exactly aligned with our supposition of bounded optimality. We feel that the promise of this early work on multitasking has not yet been fully realised in the HCI work on the topic.

The work by Hockey and colleagues on his model of "Compensatory Control" directly addressed the issues of priority and workload. Hockey's Compensatory Control theory suggests that people can manage their cognitive resources so as to preserve performance on the most important tasks in their task set, at the possible expense of increased workload and fatigue, or of secondary task performance. A series of empirical studies by Hockey and colleagues (Hockey et al., 1998; Sauer et al., 2003) tested this model using complex simulations of offices and process control settings, assigning a number of simultaneous tasks to the experimental participants. Interest focussed on the differential allocation of effort across a set of tasks given varying priorities and the effects of stressors such as fatigue or sleep loss. As predicted by the compensatory control model participants under stress successfully re-allocated effort so as to preferentially preserve performance on the higher priority tasks. No analyses of optimal performance per se were reported, but these findings certainly confirm that multitaskers cope with resource constraints by computing the relative payoff of different multitasking schedules and behaving accordingly.

More recently, a series of studies by Brumby Janssen, and colleagues has investigated similar issues in the context of dynamic dual-tasking, where one task is data entry (with a utility depending on the number of items entered) and the second task is continuous tracking (with a cost correlated with time away from task; this might be a simulated driving task or a more idealised kind of cursor-tracking) (Brumby et al., 2009, 2007; Janssen et al., 2011; Farmer et al., 2011). In a series of studies these authors have shown that people can adjust their time-sharing across such tasks according to instructional manipulation of priorities, and that when such priorities are combined into a single utility measure, concerning which the participants are given trial-by-trial feedback, performance approaches a theoretical optimum (Farmer et al., 2011).

None of this work has considered the local decision to switch from one task to another. It is interesting and important to question the function of such switches, and how they may support optimal allocation of time across a group of tasks. But beyond this, it is important to ask how a switching strategy is actually implemented by users: what kind of decision, based on what information, is the decision to switch from one task to another. In the work we review below, this decision is theorised as a variety of patch-leaving decisions, as considered in Optimal Foraging theory, as discussed at the beginning of this lecture.

S. J. Payne et al. (2007) investigated both these issues together by using a similar paradigm to the work on multiple-text browsing reviewed later in this lecture (Reader & Payne, 2007; Wilkinson et al., 2012). In that work, human browsers were free to allocate their time, moment by moment across a set of relevant texts. Accounts of the browsers' strategies assumed that they somehow monitored the rate of gain of valuable information, but evidence for such strategies remained necessarily indirect, because moment-by-moment information acquisition or learning could not be observed. Therefore, S. J. Payne et al. (2007) employed tasks for which the gain currency was observable and quantifiable to experimental participant and experimenter alike. One such task is generating words from a set of letters (see also Wilke et al. (2009)).

In Payne et al's experiments people were asked to maximise their total number of words in a fixed time; they were free to switch between two sets of letters from which words could be made. Payne et al recorded when words were generated and when participants switched. This paradigm allows exploration of the central question about discretionary multitasking raised above: why should people switch tasks, given that switching per se is likely to impose some cost?

According to our framework, the answer to this question should be along these lines: people switch because they want to maximize their overall gain (which in this case we assume is the instructed utility, i.e., the total number of words generated, although a full analysis may incorporate the cost of mental work), and because to do this they must allocate their limited time sensitively across the two tasks (the two sets of letters). Participants do not know the different gain functions of the two tasks in advance (in fact, in the experiments the sets of letters were chosen so that it was easier to generate more words from one set than the other). Consequently, it is only by working on each task and monitoring success that a multitasker can solve the time allocation problem, spending more time on the more productive task.

One simple piece of empirical evidence supports this account, but also shows that it is not the only reason people choose to switch. When participants were given a fixed budget of time for each letter-set, rather than an overall budget, they switched substantially less than when they were free to allocate their time differentially, but they still chose to switch, rather than to work on the tasks in series (S. J. Payne et al. (2007), Experiment 1).

Perhaps the primary question about participants' behaviour in conditions where they were free to allocate time differentially across the two tasks is how successfully they used this to maximize their gain. It is clear that to be successful, participants should allocate more time to the easier of the two tasks (the set of letters from which more words can be generated, or the word-search puzzle in which more words can be found), but to what extent? We suppose that the optimal solution to this problem is matching, i.e., to spend time on each task so that the overall rate of gain from each task is the same. This is optimal because both tasks will follow a diminishing returns gain curve, with different slope. If, at the end of the work period, the rate of gain on one of the two tasks is higher, more time should have been spent on that task. (Payne et al provided empirical evidence in support of this analysis.)

Beyond this broad characterisation of people's behaviour relative to unbounded-optimal behaviour, S. J. Payne et al. (2007) used the detailed timings of participants' responses and switches to test between strategies for choosing to abandon one task in favour of the other. In particular, they considered rules of thumb that biologists have found to explain patch-leaving decisions in animals (heuristics that may approximately compute Charnov's Marginal Value Theorem (Charnov, 1976), see the Introduction, given certain environmental constraints).

Patch Potential

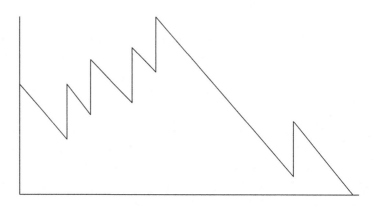

Time in Patch

Figure 4.1: A graphic representation of Green's Assessment Rule (after Stephens & Krebs (1986)). An estimate of patch potential is tracked, and the patch is abandoned when the estimate is zero. Potential decreases linearly with time, but increases by a fixed amount with every encounter with a utility-bearing item.

Across a series of experiments, using the "Scrabble" task and a quite different word-search puzzle, S. J. Payne et al. (2007) found they could predict switch behaviour quite well using a heuristic called Green's Assessment Rule (R. F. Green, 1984). This rule assumes that people will be prepared to spend a certain amount of time on a task, even if the gain is zero. However, each time a unit of currency is gained, the remaining time before a leave decision is incremented by a fixed amount, acknowledging, as it were, a more optimistic estimate of the potential of the task. (The model thus has two free parameters to predict the time spent on any one task before it is abandoned.) Figure 4.1 shows a graphical representation of Green's rule, adapted from Stephens & Krebs (1986). What Green's rule allows, without any complex mental computation, is behaviour sensitive to marginal rate of return. It therefore offers the possibility of approximating an unbounded-optimal strategy (e.g., Charnov's Marginal Value rule in the case of single-visit movement through patches) with constrained information processing.

In fact, though, Payne et al found that predictions of behaviour could be improved by assuming an additional probabilistic basis for leave decisions i.e., people sometimes chose to leave a task immediately after generating a word. This seems like a laboratory analog of the behaviour observed by González & Mark (2005), namely, changing tasks at "natural transitions" such as subgoal boundaries. As mentioned above, such a strategy may be considered generally adaptive in that it minimises switch costs. A considerable body of experimental evidence has shown that externally imposed interruptions are less costly if they take place during subtask boundaries (Adamczyk & Bailey, 2004; McFarlane & Latorella, 2002). Thus, choosing to switch immediately on subtask completion will be adaptive in terms of minimising cost.

However, paradoxically, if subtask completion were the only trigger of switching behaviour it would, in some situations, lead to maladaptive time allocation, because there would be a higher tendency to switch out of tasks with many subgoal successes. Thus, a mixed strategy, in which switching is controlled by the marginal rate of success *and* the completion of subtasks is indicated. To fully understand a complex mixed strategy requires a deeper understanding of the uncertainty (with respect to gain curves and their projection) under which the participants are working.

We believe that an Adaptive Interaction approach to the study of multitasking shows considerable promise. In the future, we hope to see approaches that combine the foraging perspective of our approach with a more detailed analysis of the variety of tasks in terms of their gain curves, and in combination with the insights that are possible from the literature on task scheduling, as argued for in the work of Moray and colleagues (Moray et al., 1991; Dessouky et al., 1995) and also, Feigh et al. (2012).

CHAPTER 5

Movement Planning

Human-computer interfaces are richly endowed with push-buttons. Buttons, virtual or otherwise, mouse-driven or touch-sensitive, are universal to contemporary computing interfaces. Buttons vary in their function and visual representation but share the requirement that some combination of perception and movement is used in order to control interaction in pursuit of goals. Most often visual perception is combined with a manual system consisting of some combination of arm, hand, and finger. Understanding interaction therefore requires an understanding of the constraints imposed by the use of the human perceptual-manual system.

Traditionally in HCI a user's movement to a button has been understood with Fitts's Law (Fitts, 1954; Card et al., 1983; MacKenzie, 1992). This is a law that, amongst other purposes, can be used to calculate a prediction of a movement time given certain constants and given the distance to, and width of, the button. It has been a mainstay of HCI research on button selection. However, the Adaptive Interaction framework demands a different approach. While some of what we present below has been anticipated and presented as variations of Fitts's Law (Welford et al., 1969; Meyer et al., 1988; Guiard et al., 2011; Jagacinski & Flach, 2003) we believe that the current landscape is sufficiently confusing, and that the modifications of Fitts's Law are sufficiently great, that it makes tutorial sense to start our description afresh. For this reason, we describe a simple optimal theory of perceptual-manual control for button selection without, in the first instance, reference to existing theory. We will return to Fitts's Law and to more recent contributions at the end of this section. We will also return briefly to the potential of more comprehensive control theoretic accounts of sensorimotor control (e.g., Jagacinski & Flach (2003)).

Here we show that the Adaptive Interaction framework can be used to answer two questions about button selection. Both answers rely on the assumption that human movements are made so as to optimally compensate for intrinsic noise in the motor system (Maloney & Mamassian, 2009; Faisal et al., 2008; Roberts & Sherratt, 1998a; Harris & Wolpert, 2006). The first question concerns where people aim. It might seem obvious that they should aim at the centre of a target, but there is evidence that this is not the case. The second question concerns how long is taken to make the movement to the target. It is believed that people will adjust the time taken to make the movement so as to trade speed for accuracy. We deal with each of these questions in-turn.

5.1 WHERE TO AIM?

To predict where a person will aim we must first understand how the selection of a button is a function of intrinsic variability in human movement. When a person moves a mouse pointer to a target point, or when they move their finger to a place on a touch sensitive display, the actual place that the pointer/finger ends up will vary across repeated trials. Moreover, this variability will be greater with faster movements than it is with slower movements.

Variability in movement is caused by a range of properties of the neural information processing system and its interfaces to the world. These need not concern us at length but it is worth setting the scene. The cognitive neural system is subject to noise, which is random disturbances of signal. Vision, for example, is limited by environmental noise that affects the rate at which photons arrive on the retina. Subsequently, perceptual amplification processes in the visual system can add further noise, and noise in neuron firing is also relevant. Further, to generate movement, neural signals are converted by mechanical forces in muscle fibers, which are further subject to noise (Faisal et al., 2008). Together, these various contributions of noise, and others, lead to trial-to-trial variation. Arguably, in fact, noise is the fundamental constraint on the performance of perceptual-motor tasks in Human-Computer Interaction.

The consequences of noise can be understood by considering the scatterplot of simulated movement end points in Figure 5.1A. The goal was to select the "Guardian" button and each black dot represents one attempt. Most of the end points result in the desired selection but some result in no selection, and one results in the selection of "Settings," to the left. The spatial distribution of the end points in the x-dimension is represented with a Gaussian density function in Figure 5.1B. The consequences of noise are normally distributed movement end points and at least two types of error.[1] Figure 5.1C is a scatterplot for a faster movement to the button. Here the movement variance is greater and the density function is more spread-out (Figure 5.1D). While it is again the case that the "Settings" button was selected once in error there are more misses to the right of the desired "Guardian" button than there were with the lower variance case.

The two types of error that are the consequence of a movement end point that is not within the bounds of the target button each have a different cost to the user. Simply missing the desired button, but not accidentally selecting another button, means that at least one more movement and selection is required to achieve the goal, though this movement will also be subject to noise and may itself result in an error that needs correction. In contrast, missing the desired button and selecting an adjacent button, in this case "Settings," will have greater temporal consequences, as the effect of this error will need to be undone before a second attempt can be made to select the desired button.

The effect of the cost of an adjacent button on selection can be understood by considering studies of optimal pointing (Trommershäuser et al., 2003, 2009, 2008; Maloney & Mamassian, 2009; Maloney et al., 2007). Rather than ask participants to minimise a utility function with a temporal currency, Trommershäuser et al. (2003) used a financial currency. They studied participants who acted to maximise financial gain in a task where they used a finger to point at a reward region, similar to a button, and avoid a penalty region, similar to an adjacent button. They demonstrated that variance, spatial layout, and the magnitude of rewards and penalties could be used to precisely predict targeting. Participants adapted targeting in response to changes in the degree of proximity

---

[1]The analysis can be extended to two dimensions, see Trommershäuser et al. (2003).

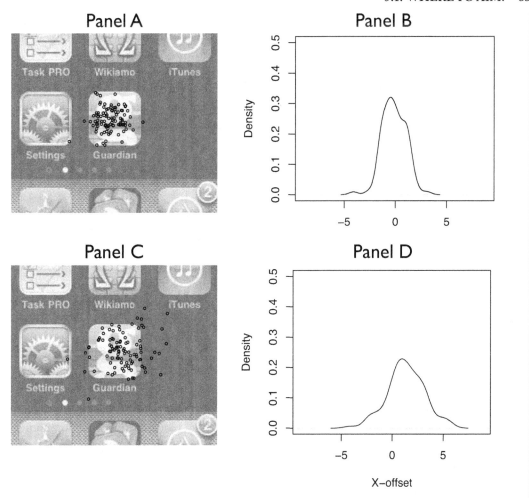

Figure 5.1: The consequences of noise on simulated movement end points while selecting buttons on a touch screen. (A) scatterplot with low noise. (B) density plot of the data in A. (C) a scatterplot with high noise. (D) density of C.

of the centres of the reward and penalty regions, and also in response to individual variations in the noise in the psychological processes used to make the required motor movements. Responses had to be rapid (under 700ms) or a penalty was incurred. If participants touched the target region then they received, say, 10 cents, the penalty region, say, -2 cents, and if they missed altogether then they received no reward for that trial. In circumstances where the reward and penalty regions partially overlapped, or were close together, then, sometimes, it made sense to aim away from the centre of the reward region. Trommershäuser et al. precisely calculated each individual's optimal aim location given the proximity of the reward and penalty regions, their magnitudes, and crucially, the spatial variance in the individual's targeting performance. Individuals with high variance needed to aim further away from the penalty region than those with low variance. The analysis confirmed that each individual did not merely change behaviour in response to their experience, but rather they selected an aim point that was optimal given their own particular experience of spatial variance. This phenomenon is illustrated in Figure 5.1C and 5.1D where the aim point, i.e., the mean of the distribution, has been offset to the right, i.e., away from the "Settings" button.

5.2   HOW LONG TO TAKE?

Having understood the impact of perceptual-motor noise on targeting location, we can now investigate its implications for movement duration and also investigate the possibility that people exert strategic control over variation. Importantly, the amount of time that a person takes to make a movement is a strategic choice. A person can choose to move quickly or slowly, and this choice has consequences. In particular, it is known that the amount of variation in the end-point movement location is related to movement duration. A person can reduce the amount of variation in the spatial location of the movement end point at a cost of spending more time to make the movement.

For this reason, if we want to predict movement duration with an optimality analysis then we need to know how variability in targeting changes with movement duration. If we apply Weber's Law then we can predict that end point variation will decrease as movement duration increases. Welford et al. studied participants performing a movement task and averaged together the distance of the end-point from the target over 100 trials for each participant to give a measure of variation that they refer to as scatter (Welford et al., 1969). They plotted movement duration against the log of scatter and fitted a linear regression. Welford et al. (1969) suggested that there is a linear relationship. Accordingly, movement duration has a negatively sloped linear relationship to the log of the variability in the end point of the movement.

Supporting evidence is available from neuro-physiological studies. It is known that the variability in force that is produced by the muscular system is proportional to the average force that is produced by the muscles (Jones et al., 2002; Schmidt et al., 1979). As movement duration is related to the force applied by the muscles (shorter durations for a fixed distance require more force), spatial variability in movement end-point will be proportional to the average forces that are generated by the muscles in making the movement and therefore inversely proportional to some function of the time taken for the movement.

In addition, the movement of arm, hand, and finger is under on-going, though not continuous, control supported by information from the perceptual system, including visual and proprioceptive information. The strategic control of movement is not about choosing a single force at the beginning of the movement and then letting the consequences for the resulting ballistic movement unfold, although some subparts of the movement are thought to be ballistic. Rather, feedback about the actual consequences of movement choices are used in a closed-loop control system.

The task for a person moving a finger or a pointer to a button is to choose the muscular forces that will cause a movement with the desired duration and desired spatial variation. It is generally assumed in design that faster is better but it is also the case that lower variation is better. There is therefore a trade-off. In order to understand this trade-off we need to understand the potential consequences of high variation. As with Trommershäuser et al.'s analysis of targeting location (above) one consequence of high spatial variation is an increased potential for the desired button to be missed, and another is for a miss combined with the erroneous selection of an adjacent button. In order to explain the movement duration we need to optimise a utility function that is sensitive to misses and errors caused by spatial variation.

Here we assume that time is the utility currency and that the range of muscle forces that can be applied constitutes the strategy space. Further, we assume that the person chooses a strategy S so as to minimise the sum of the expected movement duration T and the average time cost of errors and misses E.

$$S = \arg\min_{S}(T_S + E_S)$$

The value of E_S can be calculated given assumptions about (1) the probability of error and (2) the costs of error. The probability of an error can be determined given that the distribution of end points is Gaussian with variance determined by Weber's Law (as described above). The cost of an error can be determined given that the time to recover from the error is a function of $T_{S'}$, where S' is the strategy used to make a selection after an error. The form of this analysis would be exactly the same as that for calculating where to aim (see Figure 5.1 above).

The predicted movement duration T_S can be calculated for a desired end point variation using an equation similar to that proposed by Welford et al. (1969) but adapted to give values for a strategy S.

$$T_S = b \, log \frac{D}{V'_S} \quad + \quad (b - a) \, log \, C$$

Where b and a are constants and D is the average distance from the starting point to the end point of the movement (note that it is not the distance from the starting point to the centre of the target, or any other fixed external reference point.) V'_S is a measure of the variability for strategy S.

The equation makes the assumption that the movement consists of two submovements, which in general does not have to be the case. The first submovement, $b \, log \frac{D}{V'_S}$, is ballistic because a person first makes a submovement aimed at finishing in the rough vicinity of the target. For this first submovement, more time is required for a movement that covers a greater distance with less variance.

The second submovement duration is given by $(b - a) \, log \, C$. It captures Weber's Law and represents the time required to make a small submovement under continuous visual control.

$$C = \frac{V_S}{D}$$

Where V_S is the variability of a ballistic movement that would be observed with distance D. The equation for C reflects the idea that the second submovement should take less time after lower variance first movement.

The model assumes that V_S and V_S' are under some level of bounded control and so can be selected so as to minimise T_S.

The equations provided above are only intended as a sketch of an Adaptive Interaction approach to understanding movement for the purposes of button selection. They key idea is that noise is a fundamental constraint that results in variation but that strategies can be selected that reduce the noise at the cost of increasing movement duration. Although the idea that movement durations are maximally adaptive has been explored recently (Jagacinski & Flach, 2003; Guiard et al., 2011), disappointingly, we are unaware of any empirical evidence that tests the above model against data where participants are asked to optimise an instructed and quantitative utility function. While there are data that appear to be relevant, none of the studies provide adequate instructions concerning the utility of errors and misses. Future work should ensure that utility is controlled as it has in some previous experiments and theoretical analyses (Schumacher et al., 1999; Trommershäuser et al., 2003; Howes et al., 2009).

5.3   OPTIMIZING SUBMOVEMENTS

The model above, of the relationship between movement duration and spatial variation, did not explore the details of how a movement is controlled while in progress. There is much evidence which suggests that a movement to a button usually consists of more than one submovement and that these submovements are dynamically controlled. The submovements reflect the operation of a closed loop control system in which visual feedback and model-based movement estimation processes are used to plan and adjust the movement (Jagacinski & Flach, 2003). The stochastic optimised-submovement model captures this idea (Meyer et al., 1988). A key feature of the model is that movements are described as an optimal compromise between the durations of primary and secondary submovements. The exact form of the compromise depends on assumptions about the nature of neuro-motor noise and consequent spatial variation in the end point of a submovement.

Meyer et al.'s optimised-submovement model predicts both movement duration and error rates. The model assumes that time minimisation is achieved by adjusting the mean duration of the primary submovement and the secondary, corrective, submovement, given the size of the target and the desired error rate. If the primary submovement is too fast then the proportion of trials on which the target is missed would also be high, requiring more secondary submovements. The increased secondary submovement frequency eventually yields an overall increase in the targeting duration. Thus, to minimise the total duration of the movement, for a particular level of error, the primary submovement should not be too fast or too slow.

Currency is again total movement duration but this time given a target error rate. So the trade-off between the time cost of the movement and the time cost of errors was not made explicit but could have been. The strategy space comprises the range of target mean durations of the primary submovement.

5.4   REVISITING FITTS'S LAW

We mentioned at the beginning of the current section that some readers will be surprised that we have written about human movement and button selection in HCI without putting Fitts's Law at the centre of the analysis. For those familiar with Fitts's Law the reasons should now be clear. Where our focus has been on the strategic capability of people to choose variation in targeting in response the task constraints, Fitts's Law assumes that participants will achieve a fixed level of accuracy. Moreover, most Fitts's Law experiments, including those reported by Fitts (1954) and more recent studies by MacKenzie (1992) and Card et al. (1983) fail to impose an objective measure of utility on participants preferring instead to ask participants to perform as quickly and as accurately as possible. As a consequence, little is known empirically about the consequences of the cost of error on movement duration.

5.5   BUTTON SIZE DESIGN

An important question that might be answered with an adaptive analysis of interaction is what size to make a button. There have been studies on the effect of button size on movement time and errors (Parhi et al., 2006) but, to our knowledge, there are no models, other than developed above, that embrace the adaptive nature of human interaction.

C H A P T E R   6

Multimodal Interaction and Text Entry

Empirical studies of multimodal interaction have suggested substantial promise for improved human-computer interaction. For example, when Oviatt et al. (1997) observed participants using an experimental map device, the participants preferred to use a multimodal variant, that supported point-and-speak for spatial location tasks, over a unimodal variant. Spatial location commands, e.g., as required to add a symbol to a map, were far more likely to be completed using multimodal methods.

However, while multimodal interaction can permit multiple concurrent streams of activity, actions must sometimes be coordinated so as to generate a particular sequence or ordering. Our focus in this section is on this very particular aspect of interaction, the problem of within-mode and cross-modal response ordering. Voice recognition software, for example, may require spoken input after a visual cue is presented and before a button is pressed to confirm completion. The consequences of a set of actions will often differ depending on the order in which they are delivered. In general, the human capability to order responses is a critical requirement for interaction.

As with our previous explanations using the Adaptive Interaction framework we show that response ordering can be understood as selection of a utility maximizing strategy given constraints imposed by cognitive processing limitations that include response noise but also, here, internal noise between processes. The explanation draws primarily on work reported by Howes et al. (2009). Before we look at the structure of this explanation, we first review in a little more detail work on response ordering in text-entry. We then return to response ordering and Adaptive Interaction.

Text-entry provides what is perhaps the most obvious example of the requirement for action sequencing. Language is perfectly sensitive to order at the character level and while there are systems with auto-correct capability, generating correctly ordered character sequences remains useful(!) Text-entry systems have a long association with computing devices and this association looks set to continue into the near future. Changes in hardware, including the increased prevalence of touch-sensitive displays on smartphones, as well as advances in machine learning, mean that there are also opportunities for new designs, including, for example, opportunities for intelligent text-entry systems (Kristensson, 2009) but these too require people to be able to order action.

Empirical research on the process of text-entry, including research on transcription typing (Salthouse, 1986), has revealed many regularities, and many of these have been captured in computational models (John & Newell, 1989; Wu & Liu, 2004, 2008). Transposition errors, e.g., *hte* rather than *the* make up one of the major categories of error and they are known to occur more frequently for cross-hand sequences than within hand sequences (Salthouse, 1986). Very often, however, today's users of text entry systems probably rely on a two-thumb strategy on a miniature keyboard. While there has been much less research on the use of these systems (though see MacKenzie & Soukoreff (2002); Clarkson et al. (2005)) they too are likely to be associated with some level of transposition error, even if the frequencies of the error differ from full keyboard, skilled, transcription typing.

Transposition errors are, of course, particularly relevant to understanding how people maintain ordered responses, being, as they are, evidence of failure to maintain order. One possible explanation for the high frequency of cross-hand transposition errors is that the inter-response interval is much shorter for cross-hand than for within-hand keystrokes and therefore temporal variation in the overlapping cognitive and motor preparation processes for each keystroke can cause response reversal. However, the evidence concerning whether cross-hand inter-response intervals are shorter than within hand is mixed (Salthouse, 1986).

Another relevant effect in transcription typing is known as the preview effect (Salthouse, 1986). The inter-response interval is substantially increased by reduced preview of the text to be typed. When the letters to be typed are delivered just in time, people are substantially slower than when they can read ahead a little in parallel with typing (Coover, 1923) as cited in Salthouse (1986). The preview effect is interesting in part because it emphasises that an interactive activity such as typing is under the control of multiple neural processes that run in parallel to generate a single ordered stream of activity. Evidence suggests that the brain may be processing and preparing the hands and fingers for as many as four or five key presses ahead of any current key press (Salthouse, 1986). Skilled typists can achieve inter-response intervals of 200 ms with five, or more, character lookahead but only 700 ms intervals with one character lookahead. The fact that up to five characters may be processed in parallel, to generate a single response ordering, creates substantial opportunities for failures of response ordering.

How then do we understand text-based and multi-modal response ordering using the Adaptive Interaction framework? First, we assume that the time between any two responses is a strategic response constrained by the cognitive architecture. As we have seen before, the critical constraint is variation. However, unlike with the predictions of targeting location and move duration (previous section), we are not, here, interested in spatial variation but rather in temporal variation. We are interested in how individual responses vary in time. So, in the case of expert transcription typing each keypress might be delivered at a mean rate of 200 ms but there will be substantial variation around this mean. If one keypress is particularly slow, and the following keypress particularly fast then there is a possibility of a response reversal. At these response durations people may be able to do little to limit the noise but they can adopt strategies that are sensitive to the noise. In particular, they can strategically adjust the inter-response interval and, in addition, it may be possible for them to adopt strategies that increase the correlation between the time of adjacent keypresses.

The psychological literature offers some insight into how people adjust inter-response intervals strategically. In the Psychological Refractory Period (PRP) task participants are asked to respond to

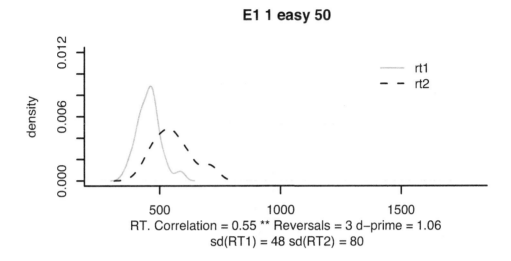

Figure 6.1: Response order density plot, after Howes et al. (2009).

two stimuli, e.g., an auditory stimulus and a visual stimulus and make a separate response to each. We will consider PRP variants in which the two responses must be ordered. Schumacher et al. (1999) report a series of experiments using the ordered PRP paradigm. Their Experiment 3 will serve to illustrate the basic structure. In this experiment participants were required to respond to a tone (Task 1) and a visual classification task (Task 2) with key presses that depended on whether the tone was high or low and whether the pattern contained a particular feature. The tone and the pattern were presented with various temporal gaps between them but here we will focus on trials in which the gap was 50 ms. Participants were asked to prioritise Task 1, i.e., to respond to the tone first and avoid response reversals. The Task 1 response times (RT1) were, on average, unaffected by the need to process Task 2. In contrast, the mean Task 2 response time (RT2), was delayed by the presence of Task 1 but the delay was less than the sum of the Task 1 and Task 2 response times when the two tasks were performed separately. Clearly, some parallelisation was used by participants, which is consistent with the preview effect in typing, but, in addition, something causes the Task 2 response to slow, suggesting that perfect parallelisation was not possible, or not desirable.

Figure 6.1 is a plot of the density functions for a particular participant in one of Schumacher et al.'s experiments. The data from over 2,000 trials are represented by the densities. They overlap, indicating that the faster responses to Task 2 were made before the slowest responses to Task 1. However, because of a correlation between Task 1 and Task 2 response times, there were only three response reversals. It is also evident in the figure that the densities are skewed, with a longer tail of responses to the right of each distribution than to the left. The long tail to the right of the Task 1 distribution accentuates the potential for response reversals.

The four experiments reported by Schumacher et al. (1999) varied in a number of respects including the modalities of the stimuli and of the required response. The individual task modalities included a visual-manual task, an auditory-manual task, and an auditory-vocal task, and different pairings were used in each experiment. Importantly, participants in all four experiments were rewarded monetarily according to a quantitative payoff scheme, and they received instruction on the nature of this payoff, and feedback, in the form of points, on their progress throughout the experiment. The currency concerned the trade-off between speed (time taken) and accuracy. Although there were small differences in the schemes, a successful pair of responses was rewarded with 100 points minus one point for every 10 ms taken to respond. Response reversals and incorrect responses were given minus 100 points. The use of this payoff scheme means that the experiment is one of the few that is sufficiently well controlled to fully test quantitative hypotheses concerning Adaptive Interaction.

As we have said, Adaptive Interaction predicts that the coordination of ordered responses to Task 1 and Task 2 is a strategic response to a utility function that precisely trades speed for accuracy, given architectural constraints. The particular models tested by Howes et al. (2009) all included noise as a key constraint, but their initial analyses indicated that while variation in response durations may be an essential component of an explanation it was not sufficient. Maximally adaptive strategies for this task that are limited only by noise in response durations turned out to generate much faster inter-response intervals than those strategies used by participants.

For this reason, Howes et al. (2009) tested models with additional constraints. In particular, it proved advantageous to incorporate interference between within-modality motor responses and interference in the cognitive response selection processes. So that while some parallel processing of responses was possible, there were limitations (see Howes et al. for a full specification). Further, following Meyer & Kieras (1997), their models correlated Task 1 and Task 2 responses by deferring the Task 2 response until after some part of the Task 1 response selection was complete.

To accomplish this analysis, Howes et al. (2009) reconstructed the ACT-R and EPIC cognitive architectures (Anderson et al., 2004; Meyer & Kieras, 1997) using a tool called CORE (Vera et al., 2004; Howes et al., 2004, 2005). CORE was designed to support the analysis of maximally Adaptive Interaction. It was used to reconstruct both the relevant aspects of the ACT-R functional architecture and the strategy space required to perform the PRP task. It would be possible in principle to perform such an analysis using ACT-R or EPIC itself, but CORE had the virtue of providing explicit support for compact generated representations of strategy spaces, and a more transparent and explicit specification of the key architectural constraints. In addition, it was necessary to modify assumptions concerning noise in these architectures. Where both architectures had previously assumed uniform noise distributions in the motor processing system (which is unrealistic), Howes et al. replaced these assumptions with more plausible gamma distributed noise. The skew in the gamma distribution reduced linearly with increased response time.

Howes et al. report payoff curves for each individual participant that plot the payoff predicted by the model against the space of plausible strategies. Plotting such payoff curves, along with the

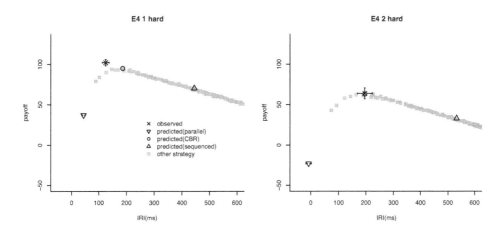

Figure 6.2: Payoff as a function of Inter-response Interval for selected individuals, after Howes et al. (2009).

observed data, is important for three reasons: (1) it allows one to see the correspondence between the optimal prediction and the actual data in the context of the theoretical payoff space; (2) it allows one to see the shape of the payoff curve that, according to the theory, participants are being asked to adapt to; and (3) it allows one to see whether the actual data is on the payoff curve, even when it is not at maximum. This provides some information about whether the participants are in fact navigating the posited payoff space, and from which part of the space they are approaching asymptote.

In Figure 6.2 the payoffs are plotted as a function of the inter-response interval for two particular participants (participant 1 left panel, participant 2 right panel). As we have said, there are two interesting predictions to consider. The first is that participant performance will correspond closely to the model inter-response interval at the highest possible payoff. The second prediction is that, even if participant performance is not at the highest value predicted, it would still be on the payoff curve. The first participant (left panel observed) performed a little better than predicted. The second participant (right panel) was exactly predicted by the peak of the payoff curve.

On average, Howes et al. report analyses suggesting that the payoff curve is a good predictor of individual performance. More importantly they report analyses that show very good R-squared values between maximally adaptive and observed Task 2 response times, and therefore, between maximally adaptive and observed inter-response intervals.

A plot of mean payoff against mean inter-response interval across participants for the fourth of the experiments reported by Schumacher et al. (1999) is shown in Figure 6.3. There are two panels in the figure, one for each of two conditions (easy/hard) in each of Schumacher et al.'s experiments. Each mean point is plotted along with the between-participant 95% confidence interval. Each panel offers predictions, with 95% confidence intervals, from the maximally adaptive model and the two

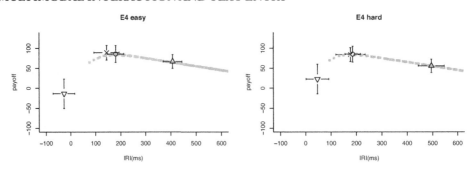

Figure 6.3: Mean as a function of Inter-response Interval, after Howes et al. (2009).

models that serve as our bound for a plausible range of behaviours: the parallel model and the serial model.

Figure 6.3 provides evidence to support the maximally adaptive hypothesis. First note that the parallel and serial models can be rejected. None of the data are in the prediction intervals of these theories. Schumacher et al. (1999)'s Experiment 4 offers a critical test of the theory owing to the absence of resource conflicts across the visual-manual and auditory-vocal tasks. It can be seen that the data are within the prediction interval of the model in both left and right panel. Experiment 4 therefore offers strong support for the maximally adaptive theory of response ordering.

6.1   COMBINING MOVEMENT AND RESPONSE ORDERING

We have now shown how Adaptive Interaction can be used to understand the strategic nature of a some basic perceptual-motor processes that are critical to nearly all human-computer interaction. Interestingly, they can be combined. While above there are separate analyses of targeting, movement, and response ordering, much interaction requires coordination of these components. For example, selecting a button requires a movement to the button followed by an action to press or push the button. It is likely that the cognitive initialisation of the push action occurs prior to the end of the movement (Gray et al., 2000) thus creating the ordering problem illustrated by the distributions in Figure 6.1. The analyses above could be combined so as to provide a more detailed account of the whole activity (M. R. Smith et al., 2008; Howes et al., 2004, 2005).

CHAPTER 7

E-commerce

When a person wants to make a purchasing decision they sometimes first gather information about the available choices. One source of information is experiential, that is, information about one's own personal experience, or in the absence of that, a person may consult the relevant experience of others. Experiential information is often solicited and propagated by interface designs, thereby facilitating a word-of-mouth network between peers (Dellarocas, 2003). Indeed, systems for providing reviews, ratings, and information about what other people like have become pervasive on the web, e.g., Amazon reviews illustrated in Figure 7.1. People use these systems to help choose clothes, movies, vacations, and even homes. They choose which stocks to invest in, and which healthcare treatments to adopt. Reading reviews and ratings allows users to engage in an ongoing process of comparison that is then terminated with a choice.

A number of studies of how people search online reviews in order to support decision making have been reported. See Lelis & Howes (2008) for an overview. There are a range of phenomena.

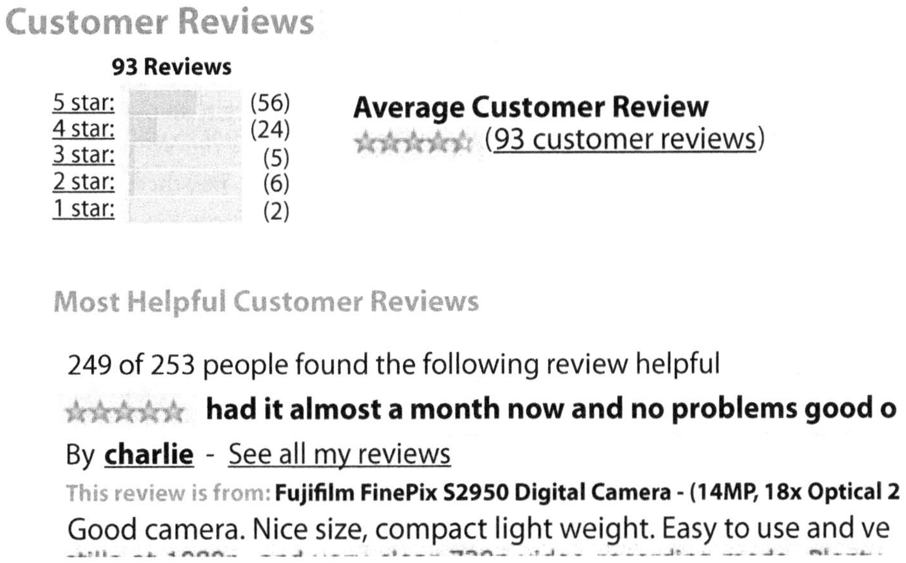

Customer Reviews

93 Reviews

5 star: (56)
4 star: (24)
3 star: (5)
2 star: (6)
1 star: (2)

Average Customer Review
★★★★☆ (93 customer reviews)

Most Helpful Customer Reviews

249 of 253 people found the following review helpful
★★★★★ **had it almost a month now and no problems good o**
By **charlie** - See all my reviews
This review is from: **Fujifilm FinePix S2950 Digital Camera - (14MP, 18x Optical 2**
Good camera. Nice size, compact light weight. Easy to use and ve

Figure 7.1: A bargraph of consumer product ratings which indexes product reviews on Amazon.co.uk. Downloaded 27th March 2012.

For example, people show a preference for negative reviews. In addition, they do not read all reviews but appear to be highly selective in choosing which reviews to read and for which products to read reviews. They read more reviews for some products than for others. The range of phenomena may reflect the dimensions of a large space of possible strategies. People appear to be exhibiting considerable choice over which reviews they read, and when. Here we consider efforts to explain these information gathering behaviours, including efforts that directly address whether the Adaptive Interaction framework has a role to play in their explanation.

An information foraging account of review foraging might start with the assumption that people are maximising the rate of information gain. The focus in such an explanation would be on optimising information, in an information theoretic sense, regardless of its purpose. This is an approach to understanding human behaviour taken by some authors (e.g. Nelson, 2008). However, as Pirolli & Card (1999) noted, "information foraging is usually a task that is embedded in the context of some other task, and the value and cost structure of information foraging are consequently defined in relation to the embedding task." Some of the time, the embedding task is a decision making task. A critical aspect of an optimality account is therefore the assignment of value to information.

In fact, determining the value of information to decision making is not straightforward and there has been much debate in the literature. We will consider three accounts and attempt to articulate the different ways in which they deal with utility and currency, with the strategy space, and with constraints.

1. The Expected Value of Sample Information (EVSI) values information to the extent that it is likely to cause a change of preferred choice (Hagerty & Aaker, 1984). This occurs when a person's top ranked alternative is replaced by another. One interesting, and clear, prediction of EVSI is that there is benefit in reading negative reviews of what appears to be the best choice. Reading a negative review of a currently favoured alternative gives a good chance of a preference reversal especially in an environment, such as the WorldWide Web, where the distribution of reviews is skewed towards positive reviews, i.e., there are many more positive reviews than negative reviews (Lelis & Howes, 2011).

   However, despite this explanation based on an optimality analysis, the human data do not support EVSI. It turns out that people favour negative reviews irrespective of their current evaluation of the product utility (Lelis & Howes, 2011). Yet according to EVSI there is no benefit in reading a negative review (a review likely to lower the expected utility) of a less favoured choice—because doing so cannot possibly cause a preference reversal.

   As ever in such cases, one possible conclusion that has proved tempting is that people are not optimal, see for example Chase et al. (1998), another is that optimality analysis cannot be used to explain human behaviour (Simon, 1992). However, an alternative is to conclude that the analysis was based on an inadequate understanding of the constraints. Taking this path, EVSI illustrates a frequently repeated error in optimal accounts of human behaviour, that is the failure to consider performance-critical constraints. It is known, for example, that people are sensitive to time costs during decision making (J. W. Payne et al., 1988). EVSI, however, is not. Any claim that a theory is optimal, demands the response, optimal given what? And if the answer is, optimal given unbounded space and time then the theory is unlikely to offer a viable theory of human behaviour. Conversely, any claim that a behaviour is suboptimal demands the response, suboptimal given what? And if the answer is suboptimal given implausible constraint or currency assumptions then the problem is with constraints or currency not the optimality assumption.

2. The Discriminating Value of Information (DVI), motivated by Harvey & Bolger (2001), provides a descriptive account of the value of information in which information is valued more highly to the extent that it separates the estimates of the utility of each choice. Information that is expected to increase the difference in utility of two choices is valued more highly. DVI is attractive empirically because, for example, it captures the fact that participants appear to seek negative reviews irrespective of whether they are for the best or second-best alternative (an observation not explained by EVSI).

In an environment with many more positive reviews, a negative review for either the favoured or the second-best alternative can increase discrimination (Lelis & Howes, 2011). When there are many positive reviews the expected value of each choice tends to be high. For the best choice a negative review has a chance of both causing a preference reversal and at the same time causing an increase in discrimination (Lelis & Howes, 2011). For the second-best choice a negative review will tend to increase the discrimination without changing the ranking.

However, while DVI offers a good description of this aspect of the existing data it does not offer a quantitative explanation for *why* people should seek information that cannot cause a preference reversal.

3. An Adaptive Interaction approach to this problem, proposed by Lelis & Howes (2011), is concerned with how information, and therefore search for reviews, is shaped by expectations about the value of information to the embedding task (as operationalised in the two models above) and by the effort required to gather information. The model assumes that people might value information to the extent that it contributes to the overall utility of the decision performance. This model distinguishes between expectations about the utility of alternatives and expectations about the value of information, and examines the relationship between them. Lelis & Howes (2011) studied the value that people ascribe to information that they gather through this process. Following J. W. Payne et al. (1988); J. W. Payne (1996), they proposed that people collect information so as to optimise the value of the decision outcome offset by the costs of the decision process.

Lelis & Howes (2011) were particularly interested in the effect of prior expectations concerning the utility of the choices on which alternative people decide to find out more about. More specifically, they were interested in whether people look for information about the stronger, currently preferred alternative, or its weaker alternative. The question here concerns the effect of prior utility on information gathering actions.

In contrast to EVSI, Lelis & Howes (2011) propose that people are maximally adaptive review readers given a thorough analysis of the human constraints. In contrast to DVI, the purpose was not to describe the human data but rather to explain the information gathering strategies that people adopt as maximally adaptive consequences of invariant constraints on human information processing and experience. However, the Lelis & Howes (2011) model is a work in progress and further development of its quantitative basis is required.

7.1   STRATEGIES IN DECISION MAKING

EVSI or DVI are sometimes described as decision strategies and the scientific problem is sometimes cast as finding *the* decision strategy favoured by people. However, the strategy that a person adopts depends on the constraints. The utility of strategies will vary depending on individual differences in constraints and variation in their experience of the task environment (for example the experienced skew in the distribution of reviews). Therefore, rather than ask which strategy people choose we can ask which strategy should they choose given individual and local constraints. In order to answer this question it is necessary to consider the entire constrained decision problem and ask how strategies can be derived from theories of these constraints.

7.2   APPLICATION TO DESIGN

If an optimality analysis can be deployed to understand the use of reviews, can it also be used to inform design? Making use of a theory of utility and currency assumptions, the optimality principle, and an analysis of the plausible strategy space it may be possible to provide a computational prediction of the effectiveness of proposed designs.

One reason that optimality analysis is important to design is because an implication of the framework is that a change in design may lead to a change in strategy (Pirolli, 2007). A comparison of the relative quality of two designs cannot be achieved by comparing their performance given the same strategy, rather the strategy must be selected in response to the particular design. For example, the presence of a summary bargraph of ratings as provided by Amazon, may encourage an increase in access to negative (1*) reviews and/or it might change the time cost of accessing reviews. Other outcomes are possible, predicting which requires an analysis of subjective utility, of constraints, and of experience.

This Adaptive Interaction framework might help resolve one or more questions in a complex ongoing debate. Despite the prevalence of reviews on the web there is some debate about how to present them and about their value. For example, some researchers have urged retailers to artificially reduce exposure to negative reviews (Lee et al., 2008), and they have done so in the face of earlier work suggesting that transparency improves consumer experience, which in turn improves retention (Lynch & Ariely, 2000). Reflecting various academic debates, the design of consumer review sites is a continually changing landscape. Some sites allow users to quickly access negative reviews while others do not. Some sites provide only textual descriptions, others also provide quantitative rating. Some provide long lists of reviews in chronological order, others are more selective. Some provide a rating mean and others provide a distribution. Some retailers provide consumers with the option of rating the helpfulness of a review, and others do not. Indeed, there is an active research field investigating how to design for effective consumer reviews (Lelis & Howes, 2008, 2011).

To close this section, we observe that it has long been know that designing web sites so that they support decision making, e.g., a choice between products, requires more than a logical organization of information, with meaningful link labels (Lohse & Johnson, 1996; Miles et al., 2000). Rather, what is needed is functionality that allows users to compare and contrast alternatives so as to maximise the utility of the decision outcome. One step towards achieving this functionality may be developing theories that explain human choices concerning information that start with the assumptions of the Adaptive Interaction framework.

CHAPTER 8

Browsing Multiple Documents and Skim Reading

Although the framework of adaptive interaction is geared to making quantitative predictions about user strategy that can guide design, the same framework can motivate qualitative accounts—and this may be a necessary avenue of progress in task arenas where quantitative utility functions are difficult to specify or estimate.

This much is true concerning what is perhaps the most commonplace interaction between humans and computers—reading text on-line. Whatever a reader's goals, the web contains an over-abundance of relevant or distracting text. It seems unsurprising, therefore, that many studies of on-line reading show how prevalent is skim reading, i.e., selectively scanning and reading from a document, devoting considerably less time to it than it would require to read linearly from beginning to end (e.g., Liu, 2005; Morkes & Nielsen, 1997).

From the perspective of Adaptive Interaction, if skim reading is widespread, we assume it is optimal, given the reader's cognitive limitations and experience and the utility of reading (Figure 1.1); people skim read because it is better than any other reading strategy given the ecology of online text. Skim reading, we assume, provides a way of allocating limited time to good documents among the plethora of good documents, and to good parts of documents which there is not time to study at length. Structurally, the problem of allocating time preferentially between documents, or between parts of a document, has something in common with the problem of allocating time across tasks in multitasking situations and, to anticipate our conclusions, the same decision-making strategy has some explanatory purchase.

But from this point of view the rather small experimental literature in cognitive psychology on skim reading poses a challenge: the papers published prior to the work of Reader & Payne (2007) and Duggan & Payne (2009) all seemed to suggest that people were unable to skim read effectively, i.e., unable to allocate their attention selectively to the most important parts of a document for their goals. The most important and influential study is that of Masson (1982a) (see also Masson, 1982b), who tested participants' recognition memory after reading through short documents of between 400 and 1000 words at various rates. The recognition tests included statements from the studied documents that were either "important" or "unimportant" or required inferences from the reader. Participants had to distinguish these statements from false statements that were created by taking statements from the documents and altering their meaning.

Recognition tests were analysed using Signal Detection Theory (Section 3) to separate discrimination from bias. Results showed that readers' recognition accuracy deteriorated as reading rate increased, and, crucially, that this deterioration was roughly equal for all sentence types. If skim reading were an adaptive behaviour one would predict that recognition of important sentences would be relatively preserved. Studies since Masson (1982a) have used a similar experimental logic, and similarly found little evidence for effective skimming (e.g. Carver, 1984; M. Dyson & Haselgrove, 2000; M. C. Dyson & Haselgrove, 2001; Kiwan et al., 2000).

Following Duggan & Payne (2009), we suggest that the logic of these experiments is correct, but insufficiently sensitive to uncover the adaptive qualities of skim reading. In particular, the use of short narrative texts seems to us a strange choice: skim reading is perhaps more adapted to longer, expository texts, where the relation between facts is more a matter of logic and less determined by chronology and happenstance, allowing better inferences concerning the content of unread sections.

In this section we review work which takes a different approach. First, in the studies by Reader & Payne (2007) and Wilkinson et al. (2012) readers are presented with multiple documents, so that the purpose of skimming is to allocate time adaptively across these documents, and the question is whether people can achieve this, and if so, how. Second, in the studies of Duggan & Payne (2009) and Duggan & Payne (2011), skim reading within a single document is tested by giving readers limited time and asking if they can nevertheless benefit from having a whole document available, rather than simply having their reading interrupted. Both sets of studies report the prevalence of an interesting cognitive strategy for time allocation, that is a form of "satisficing" (Simon, 1957) and which is the focus of our review below.

8.1   BROWSING MULTIPLE TEXTS

The general problem addressed by Reader & Payne (2007) is closely related to the central concerns of one of the analytic frameworks germane to Adaptive Interaction—namely optimal foraging theory, and in particular its extension to information foraging by Pirolli & Card (1999).

Consider, for example, an informal study described by Pirolli & Card (1999). MBA students were observed as they gathered source materials and made notes for a writing assignment. Their first activity was an electronic keyword search which retrieved 300 citations, far more than the students had time to read. Subsequently, the students engaged in a series of "triage" activities to select the most relevant (c.f. Buchanan & Loizides, 2007; Buchanan & Owen, 2008). Rapid judgment of titles reduced the list to 51 citations that were printed. The students met in a group conference to categorize these articles under nine important topics, which in turn were used to choose 27 representative documents that were collected and read. A further nine articles were rejected during this phase, leaving the students with 18. Throughout this process the students were evidently primarily driven by judgments of topic relevance, made on the basis of document titles and summaries and based on a schema derived from the content of their assignment. A substantial body of HCI research has investigated how documents might be presented to allow such relevance-based filtering (e.g. Cockburn et al., 2005).

It seems possible in principle that rapid judgments of the relevance of documents or document sections might be the primary cognitive process that underpins skim reading, but the research we wish to review here finds a rather different strategy to be important. According to the Adaptive Interaction framework, a strategy for selective allocation of time and effort to texts or to subsections of a text should be chosen so as to maximise the utility of reading effort. However, it is rather difficult to measure the utility of reading, even if readers presumably have some access to how much they are learning as they read.

Thus, we are as yet unable to consider in-principle-optimal behaviours, and test the properties of observed behaviours against these ideal solutions. Instead, to study multiple-text browsing, we consider behaviour to be adaptive to the extent that it is better (i.e., it returns more utility) than a simpler behaviour that is insensitive to the particular environmental properties (the qualities of the available texts). This is the approach taken in our empirical work, with respect to browsing, because we do not know what constitutes optimal time allocation across texts, but can assume that an adaptive allocation will be sensitive to the relation between a participant's expertise and the difficulty level of the text. In other words, for this task Reader & Payne (2007) adopted a relatively permissive definition of utility. Their primary concern was not with distinguishing the details of how skim reading strategy might be adapted to internal information processing constraints, including memory, instead their focus was on adaptation to relatively large changes in the external environment, such as the order in which documents were presented in a browser, and whether or not a document summary was visible. In the work on skim reading within a single document, the approach is rather to measure participants' learning after skim reading, and to compare this with learning from linear reading.

For time allocation in multi-document reading to be adaptive, readers must be sensitive to the differences among the documents in terms of how much learning each is likely to support. However, readers may find this quality of documents difficult to judge. Furthermore, even in cases where individuals can assess the suitability of documents with some degree of reliability, such assessment may require time that would better be spent studying. And even if documents have somehow been ranked accurately, it is not clear that the reader should spend all their time in the best document, because other documents may contain unique, valuable information (see Rouet et al. (1997)). To begin to study this complex set of issues, Reader & Payne (2007) allowed readers to browse freely among a small set of online documents that were all equally relevant to the readers' goal but varied in difficulty level, so that for a given reader some texts were indeed better than others in terms of the learning they supported.

The effects of text difficulty on learning were the subject of a study by Wolfe et al. (1998). In the terms of contemporary theory of text comprehension, learning from text requires the construction of a "situation model" mental representation of what the text is about. Because construction of a situation model depends on the overlap between the text content and the individual's prior world knowledge, it follows that the learning utility of any text will depend on a person's expertise. If there is too much overlap between the text and the reader's background knowledge, then the text provides too little new information. On the other hand, too little overlap would make the text too difficult to comprehend. Thus, the best texts fall in the middle ground that Wolfe et al. (1998) call the "zone of learnability." (Metcalfe (2002) presents a similar construct also inspired by Vygotsky that she calls the region of proximal learning.) The study by Wolfe et al. broadly confirmed these predictions. They used four expository texts about the human heart, which varied in level of difficulty from an introduction for elementary school children to a medical school text. Participants were either non-medical students or medical students. After a pre-test for knowledge about the heart, participants were assigned one of the four texts chosen at random. The amount learned from reading was assessed by the difference between post-tests and pre-tests and between post-essays and pre-essays. Wolfe et al. reported that students learned best when they were assigned a text with content that overlapped at an intermediate level with their background knowledge. It follows that at least one adaptive approach for time-limited readers would be for them to focus their time and resources on texts that they judge to be within the zone of learnability.

8.2   THE STRATEGY SPACE

In most of the quantitative domains we have considered and reviewed above, it makes sense to regard a "strategy space" as the space defined by parametric variation in a strategy. But in general, and particularly in less well understood domains there may be a need first to consider qualitatively separate strategies (each of which defines a space, according to its effective parameters). We believe that skimming is just such a case, and will outline two qualitatively distinct strategies. These strategies differ most crucially in the extent to which they separate or integrate exploration versus exploitation of unknown resources.

8.2.1   A SAMPLING STRATEGY

Sampling is the term used in the behavioural ecology literature for a strategy of rapidly assessing food-patches before settling down to exploit the patch with the highest energy content (Krebs et al., 1978). Sampling is clearly very closely related to the idea of document triage—the rapid assessment of document relevance. We prefer the term "sampling" because we wish to label the behavioural strategy of rapid judgment in advance of acceptance (use) or rejection, without presupposing that relevance is the only property which such judgments might consider.

A reader allocating limited time among a number of documents may first sample the documents, perhaps inspecting headings or particular paragraphs—just as the MBA students studied by Pirolli & Card (1999) were observed to do. In this phase of activity the primary goal is not to learn about the topic, although some learning will take place, but rather to learn about the documents. When all documents have been judged, the individual chooses the best document to read. Once this document has been read to the individual's satisfaction, he or she may, if time allows, move to the next best text or re-sample the remaining texts. Such an iterative method of sampling might be preferred because information needs are likely to change after reading any relevant text. The sampling strategy has the benefit of allowing, in principle, a browser to discover the best text for their purposes, but has costs of lost opportunity because time is spent exploring and judging that could be spent reading to learn (although against this, it is possible that sampling additionally allows construction of preliminary mental scaffolding for the contents of the multiple texts).

8.2.2   A SATISFICING STRATEGY

A rather different method of attaining adaptive time allocation is to adopt a form of satisficing strategy (Simon, 1957). In Simon's initial description of satisficing, someone who wants to sell a property has to decide which bids to accept. One strategy is to set a threshold acceptable purchase price, consider each bid in order and accept the first one to match or exceed the threshold.

Similarly, suppose that before reading, the reader sets an aspiration level as to how much they expect to learn from a unit of text and that as long as a text meets that aspiration level they continue to read. If a text is good enough throughout, then ordinary "linear reading" (Foltz, 1996) will result. When current satisfaction drops below this threshold the reader would move to the next unit of text. As discussed later, if the unit of text is relatively small and the satisficing threshold is rather high, so as often to be unmet, then satisficing, conceptualised in this way, will lead to text being skimmed.

When sampling, exploration and exploitation are separated into two phased activities and there is a commitment to choose the best text available (or at least to filter and order the texts. according to their judged or predicted utility). But in our conception of satisficing, exploration is integrated into the reading process: the primary goal is always to learn about the topic, but nevertheless readers monitor how much they are learning for the purpose of study-time allocation. Furthermore, there is no commitment to finding the best text available. As long as a text is good enough to meet the learning goals, it will be read.

We should be careful to note that, from our perspective, satisficing is not to be contrasted with optimisation. It is quite possible that, given cognitive bounds, satisficing is an optimal strategy for allocating time across texts, even though it is not committed to finding the optimal text. Nevertheless, satisficing has the potential disadvantage, compared with sampling, that the individual may well spend more time in lower quality texts, but has the potential advantage that all time is spent exploiting texts and no time devoted exclusively to evaluating the texts.

Both satisficing and sampling, if supported by valid judgments of text utility, will allow more time to be allocated to better texts, and in this weak sense both can be considered adaptive. Which strategy is the better seems likely to depend on a complex configuration of issues concerning the available texts, the reader's tasks and the reader's capabilities. Eventually, we would hope that a programme of research into skim reading informed by the Adaptive Interaction perspective could offer a richer understanding of these issues.

Sampling is only possible to the extent that text utility for the task at hand can be judged reliably and quickly relative to the time available to read the texts. Sampling is likely to be better than satisficing if there is more than one text that is in some sense "good enough," and so likely to exceed the reader's prior threshold, and yet there exist significant and perceptible utility differences among the set of available texts. Unless both these conditions are met, satisficing may well be the better strategy. For example, if only one text is good enough, then the sampling strategy would inspect all texts before choosing the one good-enough text. The satisficing strategy, on the other hand, will reject texts in turn until it comes across this text after which it will exploit it without wasting time inspecting all subsequent texts. Under these circumstances sampling would only be better than satisficing if judgment of a text by sampling were significantly quicker than the decision to leave a text that drops below threshold. Likewise, if there are no important differences among the set of good-enough texts then choosing among them will be a waste of time and effort.

Of course, a reader faced with a task and a set of texts is unlikely to know which of these various situations pertains until they have initiated one strategy or another. Initial choice between the strategies, therefore, must be determined by aspects of the task in general, immediately apparent characteristics of the texts, such as the number, and by guesses concerning the likely properties of texts based on prior experience.

8.3   CORRESPONDENCE TO HUMAN BEHAVIOUR

Each of these model strategies makes distinct and testable predictions about the pattern of time allocation among multiple texts during study. These predictions have been tested in several experiments using multiple online texts by Reader & Payne (2007); Wilkinson et al. (2012). Furthermore, the satisficing strategy has been investigated in a series of studies of skim reading single documents (Duggan & Payne, 2009, 2011).

First, consider Experiment 1 of Reader & Payne (2007). Readers were given a pre-test about the human heart and then were presented with access to four separate documents, all about the human heart, using a browser interface that allowed immediate access to any of the four pages of any of the documents, via a permanently visible menu. The four documents were all relevant, but varied considerably in difficulty level, ranging from a text written for primary school students to one written for medical students. Reading time was limited to 15 min, which is roughly as long as it would take to read any one of the texts from beginning to end (texts were used, with permission, from Wolfe et al. (1998)). Participants were asked to study the texts for this time, so as subsequently to write a 250-word essay on the structure and function of the human heart.

In these circumstances, participants' browsing behaviour was relatively exhaustive and systematic, in that most people visited all four documents and very few revisited any document before all had been visited. Nevertheless, browsing was selective, in that on average participants spent almost half of their time on their own most preferred text. Crucially, there was evidence that time allocation was adaptive, in that the more expert the readers (as measured by pre-test) the more time they spent reading more difficult documents.

As for strategy, in this experiment only 2 out of 32 participants appeared to be sampling. Figure 8.1 shows the experimental protocol for one of these participants, showing that they looked relatively quickly at all four documents before settling to read one more slowly (the criterion used to classify a reader as sampling was that they should visit all four documents within the first third of the study time).

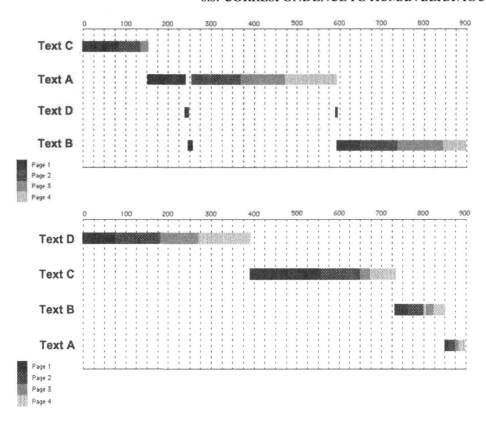

Figure 8.1: Browsing behaviour of two participants in Reader & Payne (2007) Experiment 1. The X-axis of each figure is time, the Y-axis shows the four documents in the order they appeared on that participant's browser menu (A is the easiest, D the hardest). The shaded rectangles show which page of which document was being read at every moment.

In contrast, 26 of 32 participants were classed as satisficing in that their longest visit to any document was their first visit to that document. Figure 8.1 shows the experimental protocol for one of the participants that Reader & Payne (2007) classified as satisficing. It is worth noting that this participant used almost half the experimental study time on the first document they opened, therefore with no knowledge of how good or bad for their purposes the remaining three documents might be.

Subsequent experiments (some reported in Reader & Payne (2007); others reported in Wilkinson et al. (2012)) have replicated the prevalence of satisficing as a strategy in browsing situations such as the one just described. In particular, satisficing is common and sampling rare when 8 rather than 4 texts are available, when the study goal is to study for a test rather than to write an essay, and when time-pressure is more relaxed or more severe.

When readers are allocating time across a relatively small number of texts, the only intervention that has been observed to radically increase the popularity of a sampling strategy is the provision of a very readily accessed text summary (automatically computed by presenting the first sentence from every third paragraph of the document), as in Reader & Payne (2007) Experiment 2.

Further evidence for adaptive time allocation in browsing has been shown by manipulating the expected difficulty of the post-test (which shifted preferences towards more difficult texts) and by relaxing time pressure (which also shifted preferences towards more difficult texts, presumably because more can be gained from more difficult documents if they are studied more thoroughly (Wilkinson et al., 2012)).

Satisficing is an interesting strategy in that it allows adaptive allocation of time differentially across texts without any explicit comparison of the texts and even though the utility of the texts varies in a rather subtle way. It is clearly related to the patch-leaving decision in Optimal Foraging Theory, in that it turns the time allocation problem into a single decision of when to leave the currently studied document.

8.4   SKIM-READING A SINGLE DOCUMENT

Importantly, satisficing as defined here can also apply to time allocation decisions within a single text, for example when skim reading. In a series of studies, Duggan & Payne (2009, 2011) have explored this satisficing model of skim reading.

As noted above, their studies began with an attempt to uncover a rational basis for skimming as successfully solving the reader's problem. Instead of looking for effects of varying available time-to-read on memory for important versus unimportant facts, Duggan & Payne varied the amount of text that a reader with limited time had access to. If a reader can only afford enough time to read half a document, do they nevertheless benefit from having the whole document available, so as to allocate their attention where they see fit?

Duggan & Payne (2009) found that, yes, they did. When readers were allowed about the amount of time it would take to read half an expository document they learned more from the full text than if they were given just the first or second half to study. Beyond this, Duggan & Payne (2011) used eye-tracking data to show that skim readers were able to allocate attention preferentially to the most important parts of a skimmed document, at the level of sentences (judged important or less important by independent judges).

Beyond these functional advantages of skim reading, Duggan & Payne discovered evidence that the strategy for time allocation under such conditions was a version of satisficing: readers continue to read through a section of text until learning falls below threshold, at which point they leap to the next section. As a specification of strategy this is, admittedly, rather loose. What counts as a section?

Duggan & Payne (2009) report that skim readers spent more time reading text that was earlier in a paragraph, but spend some time reading almost all paragraphs. This is consistent with a skimming-by-satisficing account in which the paragraph is treated as the patch, the unit of text to be judged, and abandoned when rate of gain is too low.

Duggan & Payne (2009) further note that more time is spent on text that is early on a page, and early in the document. They argue that this preference for early text at different levels may be understood if pages and documents suffer from diminishing returns in terms of valuable information (it must be noted here that the documents had been structured so that pages corresponded with sub-topics). Such a tendency could arise from redundancy, and from writers' stylistic tendency (recommended in many guides) to place important information early in documents and sections, with later text covering hedges and details.

Quite a different, and more complex possibility is that the satisficing strategy itself judges patches of text at different levels simultaneously. Perhaps, when a paragraph is judged as uninteresting, so abandoned very early, the judgment of the section that contains that paragraph is also depressed. This brief sketch shows how much future work is needed to fully specify the skimming-by-satisficing theory as Adaptive Interaction. We propose that such future work might be guided by a more thorough analysis of what the optimal time allocation within a document is likely to be, given the limitations on readers' comprehension skills and the utility of acquiring valuable information.

Even at the current level of understanding, Duggan & Payne (2011) propose that the theory of skim-reading by satisficing holds some practical implications for the design of online text. Among the implications they listed were the following three:

Locating information at the top of pages and paragraphs increases the likelihood of that information being read. This straightforward recommendation is not new, and indeed it may be that writers' placing important information early is the main reason for these preferences among skim readers.

Information later in a text is still read by time-pressured readers. The satisficing strategy is not equivalent to merely reading beginnings of pages or paragraphs. Rather, whole paragraphs are read when the information gain justifies that.

Skim reading is effective. Skim readers do manage to understand and remember text. When skimming by satisficing, passages of text may be read for just as long as they would be when read without time pressure. The fact that people often skim read online does *not* mean that complex information cannot be communicated in online documents.

CHAPTER 9

Adaptively Distributing Cognition

Sometimes[1] it seems that modern technologies provide such abundant resources for finding things out that it hardly seems worth remembering at all (Dix et al., 2003). Yet, as we shall see, people make choices about what to try and remember that are subtly affected by the design of devices and by the ecology of interaction.

Three separate aspects of the distribution of information between the external world and human memory seem to us crucial for understanding human-computer interaction. First is the use of computers and networks of computers for storing declarative knowledge, meaning that such knowledge can be searched for rather than remembered (Dix et al., 2003). Second is the support that the technology offers for action, in particular that it affords a style of action that we have called "display-based" (Howes & Payne, 1990; S. J. Payne, 1991; Howes, 1993; Howes & Young, 1996). Third is that these same aspects of the display allow a kind of problem solving that we call "interactive search" (S. J. Payne et al., 2000), in which the users' problem space is mapped very directly onto the computer display.

In each of these cases we will argue that, contrary to influential views in Human-Computer Interaction, the distribution of cognition between the mind and the world is another kind of strategic decision that can be understood as optimal adaptation to the constraints imposed by cognitive architecture and task environment so as to maximise utility of action.

9.1   KNOWLEDGE IN THE WORLD

Dix et al. (2003) observe that because the time costs of accessing information from the web have in some cases approached the time costs of accessing information from memory, we are seeing strategies for seeking and remembering information beginning to change. Memorisation strategies may be relatively less efficient in a world where strategies for how to find information through the web are readily available. Mobile computing may have accentuated this trend by making web-memory ubiquitously available, just-in-time, and in the context of use.

A history of the web might be cast in terms of its development through three, ultimately coextensive, geometries, as described by Dix et al. (2003). Each geometry provides a new access structure that is more efficient for people to acquire information, and each geometry, it can be

---

[1]The title of this section is borrowed from S. J. Payne et al. (2001); the section reprises and updates the argument therein, relating it to the Adaptive Interaction framework.

argued, has enabled a shift in human strategies for what to memorise. The first geometry of the web was the hypertext link structure. The web was designed as a graph and information could be acquired by following links that seemed relevant to an information need until the required information was found (i.e. 'browsing'). The effectiveness of these structures demands that the information space is designed in a way that anticipates user needs to a high degree.

The second geometry was provided implicitly by the content of pages but required the development of search engines for it to be exploited. In this geometry, two pages are related if they share the same words. Search engines gain their power, therefore, by providing a kind of content-addressable memory that is reminiscent of human memory itself (it is striking how one of the early cognitive theories of retrieval from long-term memory, the "Descriptions" model of Norman & Bobrow (1979), posited an iterative describe/retrieve cycle that is very similar to the typical cycle of key-word searching). Moreover, the proximity of pages in this structure is, by and large, emergent rather than designed, although some deliberate engineering of meta-content is possible.

The third geometry is an emergent property of user activity. Two pages are close if they are viewed by the same person, which is one basis of recommender systems.

In the terms of our framework (see Figure 1.1) while the fundamental cognitive/neural capacities of the human mind have remained unchanged, by changing the ecology of information access, the invention of these new geometries has lowered the cost of acquiring and reacquiring information, potentially, or so it appears, making internal storage and memorisation in part redundant, but at the same time demanding the acquisition of new strategies to make full use of what is now externally available.

The effects are so profound, it seems, that empirical evidence suggests that when attempting to answer hard questions, human memory is *primed* to think about the web as a way of answering these questions (Sparrow et al., 2011). For example, behavioural studies show that when people are asked "Is an ostrich's eye bigger than its brain?" their memory systems automatically prepare for using computer-based search rather than purely internal memory search. Further, when people anticipate that they will have access to computer storage in the future then they are less likely to incidentally memorise information (Sparrow et al., 2011).

This latter finding shows the close and important relation between external storage and internal cognitive memory processes. Duggan & Payne (2008) showed that knowledge of a factual domain enables more efficient retrieval of unknown information in that domain from the web. Their experiment used a very simple method. In phase 1 participants were required to complete a trivia test (on pop music or football). In phase 2 they repeated the same test, but now had to retrieve webpages on which the answers to the questions could be found. Scores on the phase 1 test predicted performance on the phase 2 test. This was true even for those items which were unknown on the phase 1 test. Those who knew more about a topic were better at finding unknown information about that topic on the web.

The everyday use of computers as information repositories also incorporates personal information management functions. This includes structures which were designed for a store/retrieve function, such as the folder structures in which people store personal files. But also, as discussed by Whittaker, Bellotti and others (Whittaker et al., 2006, 2007; Bellotti et al., 2003), email folders, because they allow messages to be stored and retrieved, are appropriated as information management tools—e.g., as to-do lists and contact lists: "Task management involves reminding ourselves of current tasks...email's conduit function leads many of us to exploit our in-box for task management. We leave information about current tasks there, knowing that when we open it and scan its contents, we'll be reminded about outstanding tasks" (Whittaker et al., 2006, 2007).

Observations such as this have led advocates of "Distributed Cognition" (Hutchins & Lintern, 1995), to suppose that "people off-load cognitive effort to the environment whenever practical" (Hollan et al., 2000, p. 181), and that systems should be designed to maximize the potential for such off-loading (Zhang & Norman, 1994). Our view, in contrast (S. J. Payne et al., 2001), is that off-loading is discretionary, and that people will off-load more or less information as a strategic choice.

Strategic use of external information is a matter of adapting to the constraints of both computer-based search and internal memory search. This much is true of the email example noted above. Whittaker et al. (2006) points out that the email inbox is a good source of opportunistic reminding because it has to be consulted for the mainstream use of email. This is in contrast to dedicated task-managements tools, which the user must deliberately choose to access.

This argument parallels the argument made by S. J. Payne (1993) in his analysis of calendar use. Payne pointed out that in routine use of a standard paper calendar, in order to schedule and enter a new appointment the user has to read, and therefore will be reminded of already-entered appointments. Many electronic designs compromise this routine opportunistic reminding, by allowing search for empty slots and/or entering appointments by directly accessing particular time slots, without browsing through adjacent slots. Payne's interviews with calendar users also revealed strategic, discretionary aspects of the use of calendars as a memory tool, with some users reporting that they would not bother to enter appointments which they were very confident of remembering.

While these observations support our general point that the use of external information is a discretionary strategic adaptation, we don't know any empirical evidence for subtle utility-maximising strategic shifts with respect to the distribution of storage of long-term declarative information between internal and external. The argument becomes clearer, and the evidence more compelling when we consider the use of external information about methods.

9.2   METHODS ON THE DISPLAY

The methods used to interact with computer systems often require recognising actions on a display, rather than recalling them. Actions are cued step-by-step by the external environment, so that the user need not remember what the required actions are. This phenomenon was first reported in a study of telephone operators by Morton (1967). Morton discovered that even experienced and frequent users of old-style British telephone dials could not recall, nor even reliably recognise, the correct layout of letters on the dial. In HCI, Mayes et al. (1988) showed that regular users of a Mac exhibited very poor recall for menu headers and menu labels—even for those headers that are ever-present on the screen. The finding of poor recall for menu labels was replicated by S. J. Payne (1991), who also reported poor knowledge for the precise effects of commonly used operations.

These findings show that expert performance is interactive, with knowledge that is vital for performance being read from the device during activity (Draper, 1986). Furthermore, this kind of interactive performance is not very well addressed by those cognitive theories, such as GOMS, which focussed on the use of remembered goal-stacks to control processing (e.g., Anderson 1983, Card et al. 1983, Kieras and Polson 1985). Rather, to understand off-loading it helps to take an Adaptive Interaction perspective.

Consider a study by Gray & Fu (2001). They studied people learning to programme a simulated VCR, in one of three conditions: one group memorised the procedure in advance, whereas two other groups could inspect the next step in the procedure by looking at a help box. For one of the two help groups, the perceptual-motor cost of consulting instructions was increased, rather minimally, by making the instructions invisible until mouse-clicked. Gray & Fu (2001) reported that the best performance, in terms of time and errors, was in the memorisation condition. More interesting was the comparison between the two help conditions. As the experiment progressed, participants in the high cost of consultation condition often preferred not to consult the help window at all, instead relying on their imperfect memory, and thus making more errors than the other help condition, who could (and did) consult the help window simply by looking at it. This simple experiment shows that people do not always choose to off-load memory demands to the environment, but weigh the relative costs and benefits of knowledge-in-the-head against knowledge-in-the-world. (Gray and colleagues have developed their research programme since this initial study, and have themselves articulated a "soft constraints" framework that has much in common with Adaptive Interaction, though see Howes et al. (2009) for some important points of contention.)

This "adaptive off-loading" perspective can explain why Morton's telephone operators did not commit the letter-layout of the dial to memory—presumably the cost of visual search was low enough to support long-term interactive skill. In contrast, touch typists do commit the layout of the QWERTY keyboard to memory, encoded in motor programmes. In turn, this is presumably because there is so much to gain in terms of speed of data entry.

Some studies, particularly Fu & Gray (2004) (but see also Fu & Gray (2006)), suggest that there is a more complex picture than is evident from the simple dichotomy between whether people routinely off-load or whether they adaptively off-load. One reason that people may off-load more than they should is because methods for device use that are more interactive are better for performance monitoring and error control. In a series of three tasks, Fu & Gray (2004) investigated whether people make less use of more specialised (and more efficient) locally adaptive procedures, while at the same time making greater than expected use (given a calculation of efficiency) of general procedures made of more interactive procedures. In one study, for example, they analysed data reported by Bhavnani & John (2000) concerning the use of CAD systems by architects with many years of experience. These were skilled users by most definitions. Bhavnani & John (2000) observed, for example, that some architects preferred inefficient procedures that involved more incremental construction and adjustment of drawings than more specialised methods that would have got the job done more quickly. Fu & Gray (2004) report a study of simulated Videocassette Recorder (VCR) use[2] in which participants were asked to set the VCR to record a number of shows. Setting a show required a subprocedure to select the channel. A general version of this subprocedure involved navigating by pressing up/down arrow keys but this meant that it would sometimes be very slow to navigate through the 63 channels. A more specialised subprocedure allowed participants to jump, a type of goto, directly to a channel number. Fu & Gray (2004) found much less use by participants of this more efficient, but more specialised and less interactive, subprocedure. One possible conclusion from these data is that procedure selection is *not* adaptive; because people off-load rather than use less interactive and more efficient procedures. Indeed, Fu & Gray (2004) do conclude that participants are suboptimal. We will return to this claim in Section 11; for now we observe that while the more interactive methods observed in these studies may appear slower than less interactive methods and therefore, from one perspective, less efficient, their selection may be explained given a deeper understanding of their costs and benefits for monitoring and error detection, as proposed by Fu & Gray (2004).

The importance of error detection, interactivity, and recovery to the utility of procedures, and therefore whether they are adaptive, is a question that is further investigated by M. R. Smith et al. (2008) and by Eng et al. (2006). M. R. Smith et al. (2008) investigated transcription typing. A key question concerns how people interleave reading telephone numbers to be entered into a database and looking at what has been typed so as to spot typos. An overly simplistic model of utility in this task might have focussed on raw sequential throughput ignoring errors and simply adding up execution times. A better model must choose how to overlap reading while typing, and how often to check for errors depending on the cost of checking and the cost of correction. M. R. Smith et al. (2008) show how the optimal strategy changes with differences in the backspace lag time (M. R. Smith et al. (2008)). The analysis shows that the extent to which off-loading is adaptive is subtly dependent on aspects of the timing of interaction (also, see Gray et al. (2000)). The work by M. R. Smith et al. (2008) was part of a series of studies reported by Alonso Vera, Richard Lewis, and Andrew Howes on a modelling architecture directly designed to facilitate reasoning about the adaptiveness of interactive procedures (Howes et al., 2004; Vera et al., 2004; Howes et al., 2005; Tollinger et al., 2005; Eng et al., 2006; M. R. Smith et al., 2008). In general, the utilities that shape human choice of interactive methods are much more subtle than might be suggested by the simple off-load-or-not dichotomy (Eng et al., 2006).

---

[2]VCRs were a device popular in the 1970s, 80s, and 90s for recording television broadcasts. They were notoriously difficult to programme.

9.3   INTERACTIVE SEARCH (PROBLEM SOLVING AND PLANNING ON THE DISPLAY)

People do not merely interact, they also think and plan. When someone runs through their agenda during their morning shower they are planning. They are using mental processes in an effort to choose and sequence what they will do at some future time.

Planning is implicated even in simple computing tasks such as constructing a slide presentation (Bhavnani & John, 2000; Charman & Howes, 2003; Fu & Gray, 2006). Laying out a slide or a figure does not merely involve acting/interacting, it involves deciding where to place which items and how to construct complex items out of elementary shapes, lines, and text. It also involves the use of strategies for copying and pasting existing material. For example, for constructing a slide that contains a large number of repeated images there are multiple strategies by which these items can be generated. The least cognitively demanding but highest time cost strategy might involve generating each item from scratch. Many people start with this strategy when first introduced to a presentation package (Charman & Howes, 2003). However, with practice, and with *reflection*, people naturally generate more efficient strategies (Charman & Howes, 2003). These include *exponential* strategies that copy one item to make two, two items to make four, four items to make eight etc., and which can save a substantial amount of time for large problems. People sometimes stumble upon these strategies by accident but they also generate them by reflecting and planning.

Another aspect of the technology's support for goal-directed activity relates to planning and problem solving rather than routine procedural skill. To return to the Dix example of hypertext geometry, a person browsing through a website, or navigating an unfamiliar menu structure, will have to choose between actions that are perceived rather than retrieved from memory. Such "interactive search" involves traversing a problem space that is represented in the technology. This much is also true of many of the simple puzzles studied in the psychology of problem solving, such as Tower of Hanoi or the Eight-puzzle, and of course these puzzles are often implemented on a computer for experimental purposes. An important distinction, however, is this: when traversing a menu structure, the user can only use lookahead over visited parts of the structure (whether during the initial search, after backup, or on subsequent traversals).

Consider a series of studies on interactive search by S. J. Payne et al. (2000). They investigated users learning to search for information by selecting a sequence of labelled buttons on idealised two-choice points (information goals and labels were taken from real websites). The main question of interest was this: how would people use recognition memory to guide their search? In particular, when searching for already-seen goals, would they prefer a label that seemed familiar, even when they could not explicitly recollect that the label was correct for the goal in question? In such cases, one might expect the user to consider only the externally available information, i.e., the semantic plausibility or "information scent" of the label (which was indeed a reliable guide, exploited by the searchers). However, it turned out that searchers were additionally influenced by mere familiarity and, further, were more influenced by familiarity to the extent that frequency of exposure was a valid index of correctness. In other words, in keeping with our framework, users were making an adaptive decision, sensitive to the statistics of the particular information environment, about how much to rely on internal memory and how much to fall back on externally available information. (For a computational model of this strategic use of memory, see Howes et al. (2002).)

How is the distribution between internal memory and external information managed when, because the effects of operations are easily computed, lookahead and planning are more readily accomplished. (As noted above, simple puzzles are often of this kind.) It turns out that such tasks are accomplished by interleaving planning and action (O'Hara & Payne, 1998, 1999). People may not plan complete sequences of actions towards a goal before acting, but nor do they issue single actions at a time. Our perspective on this phenomenon is, of course, that the extent of planning or lookahead can itself be considered as a strategy space, and the amount of planning-before-acting is a strategic choice, an adaptation to the constraints imposed by the task environment and the human cognitive architecture, so as to maximise the utility of the plan-act behaviour.

Consider empirical evidence gathered from studies in which individuals interacted with computer-based versions of puzzles. O'Hara & Payne (1998) reported four experiments which manipulated the user interface to classic puzzles that are the precursors to the more cerebral of today's phone-based games. Using the eight-puzzle, Tower of Hanoi, and the Jump-Slide puzzle they showed that when a longer keying sequence was required to make a move, participants engaged in more planning, resulting in shorter solutions and better learning about the puzzle (as shown by transfer to other versions of the same puzzle using other user interfaces).

These ideas were extended by O'Hara & Payne (1999) to a more representative HCI task. Participants had to complete letters by copying information from several source files to several destination files. The order of sub-tasks was unconstrained, but fewer operations were required if participants copied a source text to all required destinations rather than completing destination documents one at a time. If the cost of operations was made relatively high (by incorporating a lockout time), most participants discovered the most efficient strategy at some point in the experiment (but not immediately). In the lower cost condition, participants persisted with their initial, inefficient strategy. The lesson from all these studies is that people decide how much to plan, based on their judgments of the costs and benefits of planning.

CHAPTER 10

E-commerce Feedback

One of the major impacts of technology over the past 20 years has concerned the introduction of online markets. Web technologies have begun to deliver markets in a range of economic arenas (as foreseen by Malone et al. (1987)) but only where issues concerning trust can be effectively addressed (Bolton et al., 2004). One way in which trust can be established is through reciprocity. Partners build up relationships based on a shared history of economically valuable collaboration. However, effective markets must do more than support reciprocal interaction between partners. In spheres where it is important to continually trade with new partners, reputation becomes important. Designing to support reputation demands designing for Adaptive Interaction.

Typically, feedback mechanisms provide a means for the reputation of sellers, and perhaps buyers, to be communicated within a market. Modern online markets usually provide potential buyers with information about the previous behaviour of sellers. This information typically includes information about the quality of transactions that has been provided, in one form or another, by customers of the particular seller. eBay and Froogle, for example, provides seller profiles that can be inspected by potential buyers, and this profile contains summary information about customer ratings of the seller (see Figure 10.1). In general, there is a large space of possible feedback mechanisms. There is, of course, a choice about whether to provide feedback mechanisms at all, but beyond that there are subtle but important distinctions. Feedback information might, for example, contain a long-term average of the seller ratings, or it might contain only the most recent ratings. Feedback might be presented as a mean or as a distribution or it may be desirable to avoid aggregation altogether. Feedback about a particular seller might be complemented with averages for feedback across sellers (in an effort to give meaning to otherwise arbitrary averages). Feedback information might be complemented by information about how long a seller has been in the market. A web site might make access to negative feedback faster than access to positive feedback because purchasers are known to find negative feedback particularly valuable.

This design problem raises many questions, some of which were addressed by Bolton et al. (2004). Bolton et al. report an experimental study of people buying and selling products in a laboratory version of an online market. They were interested in the effects of information about a seller's past history on a potential purchaser's decision as to whether to purchase from this seller. In this section of the lecture our strategy is to focus on this single empirical study to illustrate the application of our framework to this domain. In support of our analysis we then review related aspects of the more general literature.

The first question for Bolton et al. (2004) was that of how to model utility. They constructed a quantitative specification of the costs and benefits for buyers and sellers. Both buyer and seller

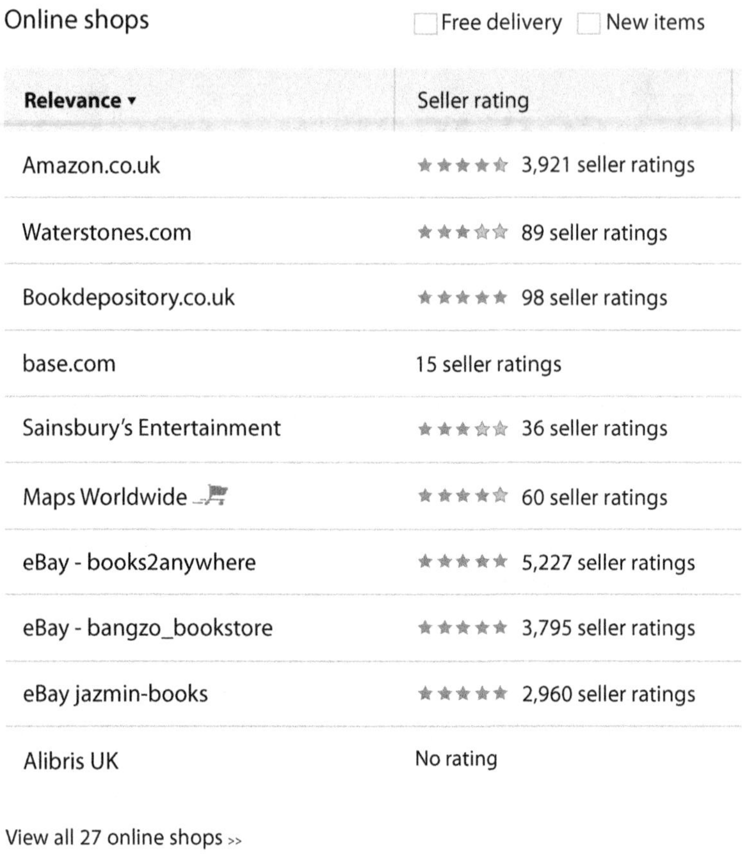

Online shops		Free delivery New items
Relevance ▾		Seller rating
Amazon.co.uk		★★★★☆ 3,921 seller ratings
Waterstones.com		★★★☆☆ 89 seller ratings
Bookdepository.co.uk		★★★★★ 98 seller ratings
base.com		15 seller ratings
Sainsbury's Entertainment		★★★☆☆ 36 seller ratings
Maps Worldwide ⌫		★★★★☆ 60 seller ratings
eBay - books2anywhere		★★★★★ 5,227 seller ratings
eBay - bangzo_bookstore		★★★★★ 3,795 seller ratings
eBay jazmin-books		★★★★★ 2,960 seller ratings
Alibris UK		No rating

View all 27 online shops »

Figure 10.1: A froogle.co.uk list of web sites showing a star rating for average customer feedback. Downloaded 27th March 2012.

were endowed with 35 units. The seller offers an item for sale at a price of 35 which has a value to the buyer of 50. The surplus to the purchaser is therefore 15. The seller's costs are 20 (these are the costs of production, selling, and shipping) and so a sale will generate a profit to the seller of 15. However, the buyer can choose not to enter into the trade, he/she can choose not to buy, and the seller can choose not to ship, i.e., the seller can accept the buyer's money without supplying the product. In this latter case the buyer receives the endowment plus the purchase price to give a profit of 70. In other words, the seller may sometimes find benefit in cheating. What is defined here is an objective utility function for the task. It is a utility function that offers a description of the observable structure of the most important aspects of the market; it defines the cost/benefit structure of trading in terms of a shared, abstract, currency of exchange. In game theory the buyer and seller are assumed to adopt subjective utility functions that correspond to this objective function and they are assumed to attempt to maximize their own personal utility.

In Bolton et al.'s study buyers and sellers were assumed to make choices so as to maximize their winnings. For the buyer, it makes sense to risk sending money for a product if they trust the seller, and for the seller it makes sense to send the product if they wish to avoid damaging their reputation, and to cheat if they think that they can do so without damaging the potential for future sales. Reputation, and the feedback through which it is propagated, is therefore critical to the operation of the market. Without it, buyers should not trust sellers and no exchanges will take place.

We will return to questions concerning strategies and constraints below. First, we review the empirical findings reported by Bolton et al. (2004). Bolton et al. were interested in how the information available to a buyer affected their decision about whether to buy. They contrasted three markets. In a stranger's market buyers knew nothing about sellers. In a partner's market buyers and sellers were paired for the duration of the study. In the feedback market buyers were randomly paired with sellers but for each pairing the buyer was provided with information about the reputation of the seller. (Importantly, in this market, feedback was always correct.)

Bolton et al. studied 144 participants (48 per market) and measured how frequently each participant chose to buy and ship products over 30 trials. Their findings can be summarised as follows:

1. The partners market was the most efficient at between 70 and 80%. The feedback market was the next most efficient at between 30 and 60%. The strangers market remained at below 30% efficiency after the first few rounds. None of the markets reached 100% efficiency.

2. Participants in the partners market were more willing to buy and ship than those in the feedback market or the strangers market, despite the fact that feedback was guaranteed to be entirely accurate.

3. The rate of shipping and of buying diminished as the final round approached.

While the findings of this study clearly favour the provision of feedback mechanisms, more analysis is required to understand the observed differences in behaviour. We provide a sketch of such an analysis here. Applying the Adaptive Interaction framework, we view the participants as utility maximizing agents who select the best possible strategies given the constraints. We have already seen that Bolton et al.'s participants were set a quantitative objective utility, with a financial currency, and there is no reason in the data to assume anything other than that the subjective utility function corresponded to the external function. The strategy space and constraints are potentially quite rich and we offer some discussion below.

Consider three types of strategy that are likely to have been deployed by Bolton et al.'s participants.

1. Defect when close to end of the relationship. Under certain assumptions, that have been influential in game theory, the optimum strategy for any individual in Bolton's task is to

defect, i.e., to avoid the risk associated with cooperative strategies. The Nash equilibrium for the purchaser is not to buy and for the seller is not to ship. However, following Goeree & Holt (2001), and others, we assume that it is evident that people can, and do, achieve higher utility with strategies that involve selective cooperation. The utility achieved by people in scenarios such as that described by Bolton is higher than predicted by the Nash equilibrium strategy. Participants do not start with perfect information about others; there may be pre-acquired tendencies to cooperate; and there are opportunities to use learning over multiple trials to coordinate (Mailath & Samuelson, 2006). However, it is also evident in Bolton et al.'s study that rates of defection do increase as the last trial of the study approaches.

2. Reciprocity strategies. The strategy space for the buyer depends on the information available about the seller. In what Bolton et al. call a partners market, buyer and seller are paired so that the buyer always purchases from the same seller. Here, the strategy for both the buyer and seller might be a version of tit-for-tat, which is believed to be optimal in many circumstances. Tit-for-tat is known to be effective in iterated Prisoner's Dilemma, the earliest task designed for studying cooperation between payoff maximising agents. Defection, i.e., cheating, is known to be the optimal strategy in the one-shot version of the game, however cooperative strategies can prosper in an iterated version of the task, i.e., when participants play the task repeatedly, particularly if participants do not know when the last trial will occur. Computational implementations of tit-for-tat, which defects after the opponent defects and collaborates after the opponent collaborates are known to perform well in tournaments (Axelrod, 1997).

There have been a number of human studies of Prisoner's Dilemma in which tit-for-tat like strategies are used voluntarily by the participants. However, it is also known that in more ecologically motivated variants of Prisoner's Dilemma participants sometimes use a strategy called raise-the-stakes (Roberts & Sherratt, 1998b). Raise-the-stakes allows for different levels of cooperation, so that a buyer, for example, can initially test a seller by purchasing low-value items and then slowly increase the value of the trades. Bolton et al.'s market did not allow participants to use raise-the-stakes but variants, including real-world online commercial environments may do so. A version of raise-the-stakes has also been observed in studies of friendship development (Hays, 1985) suggesting that studies similar to that conduct by Bolton et al. could be used to study how social network sites support, or hinder, the development of friendship.

3. Reputational strategies. While tit-for-tat is a viable strategy for social dilemmas which involve only two agents, in reality many social dilemmas, including the feedback market studied by Bolton et al., arise when many individuals interact. The key problem for agents seeking to cooperate in large groups is that it is more difficult to punish people who cheat (Boyd & Richerson, 1988; Phelps et al., 2009). Strategies like tit-for-tat or raise-the-stakes are not sufficient on their own to prevent cheating when groups are large enough that any two individuals are paired relatively infrequently. Online retail markets tend to be more similar to this than to

partners markets, although partner relationships may emerge as a strategic choice even though individuals operate within larger groups. In these circumstances people make use of the reputation of others in order to decide whether to cooperate. Reputation provides evidence about a person's previous history to an individual with whom there may not have been any direct previous interaction. Critically, reputation can result in indirect reciprocity: collaborating with strangers because they have collaborated with others. A reputational mechanism can also result in collaboration merely in order to gain a good reputation, and thereby hoping to benefit from the conditional collaboration with others in the future (Mailath & Samuelson, 2006). Nowak & Sigmund (1998, 2005) studied the effect of reputation, which they called 'image scoring', in a many-player social dilemma game using both simulation and mathematical analysis, and found that reputation plays a central role in group cooperation.

The standard analyses of the strategies deployed by people in solving reputation games, as described above, typically assume no constraints. People are assumed, falsely, to possess unbounded capacity to remember social information whether that information concerns reputation in the form of an image-score or merely a summary of the history of interaction with an individual. Stevens et al. (2011) point out however that memory is a required capacity for processing social information and that different social strategies have different memory requirements. Social strategies may therefore be misapplied due to interference between memories, or strategies that are more robust to memory interference, e.g., contrite Tit-for-Tat, may be preferred even though, in the absence of memory constraints, they would not be optimal. Some empirical evidence exists. Milinski & Wedekind (1998), for example, found that interleaving a working memory task changed the strategy used for participants who were engaged in a simple Prisoner's Dilemma like game. Others have found similar effects of memory constraint on performance in social games (Winkler et al., 2008).

Stevens et al. (2011) report an experiment designed to test whether typical decision strategies, including tit-for-tat, are cognitively feasible. They used an experimental design in which each participant experiences a sequence of simulated partners who chose to cooperate or defect. Participants' memory for these simulated partners and their decisions was tested. Participants did not actually play a social dilemma game as the study was focussed on testing memory for information required to play social dilemma decision strategies. So as to test the effects of memory interference, Stevens et al. (2011) used two manipulations. The first manipulation concerned the number of (interleaved) simulated partners. The second manipulation was of the number of interactions with each simulated partner. The first manipulation was designed to test retroactive interference, i.e., how new memories interfere with old. The second manipulation was designed to test proactive interference, i.e., how old memories interfere with new.

Stevens et al. (2011) results show that human participants have a great deal of difficulty in recalling the previous actions of simulated partners. Interference, both proactive and retroactive, has negative consequences for the recall of information that could be usefully deployed when playing social games. The conclusions that we draw from these findings are twofold: (1) feedback mechanisms need to be designed in such a way as to support memory for previous transactions. (2) models designed to predict maximally adaptive behaviour in reputational games, including those that require substantial HCI, must be sensitive to cognitive constraints.

Returning to our framework. Adaptive interaction demands that both buyers and sellers maximise utility given the cognitive and social constraints. In the market scenario described by Bolton et al. (2004) the choice, for the participant, of which strategy to adopt over trials was a utility maximisation problem limited by the available information about the individuals with whom they were trading (feedback, partners, strangers) and limited by individual memory for past history of reciprocity and reputation (Stevens et al., 2011).

The need for feedback mechanisms is clearly supported by the results of Bolton et al.'s studies but there is still an efficiency gap. Addressing real-world correlates of this gap is an ongoing design challenge.

CHAPTER 11

Discussion

The purpose of this lecture has been to explore how Adaptive Interaction, a framework inspired by Foraging Theory, Cognitive Game Theory, and Cognitively Bounded Rational Analysis can be applied to understanding interaction in a broad range of HCI tasks. When applied to HCI tasks these three frameworks amount to the hypothesis that people are maximally adaptive to utility given ecological constraints, and constraints imposed by cognitive mechanisms (Figure 1.1).

The HCI concerns that we have examined include signal detection and diagnosis, multitasking, movement planning, multimodal interaction, purchasing decision making (including the use of vendor feedback and also reviews), skim reading, memory off-loading, and planning. We have seen that for some tasks, for example, choosing the aim point of a button press, or choosing the duration of a move to a button, or ordering responses, there is a straightforward application of the framework. A detailed quantitative analysis of the utility associated with each of a set of strategies generates a predicted behaviour that, where data is available, is confirmed by the empirical evidence (Trommershäuser et al., 2003; Meyer et al., 1988; Howes et al., 2009; Swets et al., 1961). For other tasks, such as skim-reading, a more qualitative application of the framework has been used because of current difficulties, which are not necessarily insurmountable, associated with the measurement of priors and measurement of the value of information.

We have also seen that the framework can be applied to both individual and collaborative tasks. Individual tasks include button pressing, reading product reviews, and skim reading. Collaborative tasks include diagnosis by teams and selecting vendors on the basis of reputation. A number of modelling approaches are available to help understand these different kinds of task. Decision theory plays a critical role in modelling button pressing, as it does in Signal Detection Theory (SDT). Game theory plays a critical role in explaining the role of reputation in the selection of a vendor and therefore in the design of feedback mechanisms. However, all of these modelling approaches share a commitment to the three components of the Adaptive Interaction framework. They all demand a quantitatively specified decision problem, they all demand a commitment to a utility function expressed in terms of a particular currency, and they all demand a commitment to a set of information processing constraints that delimit the space of possible strategies.

11.1 ISSUES FOR OPTIMALITY AND ADAPTIVE INTERACTION

For many, the question of whether Adaptive Interaction provides a coherent framework for understanding Human-Computer Interaction will hinge on the plausibility of the optimality assumption.

We recognise that the assumption that people routinely find optimal, utility-maximising strategies, given the constraints imposed by cognitive mechanisms and the experienced ecology, remains highly controversial (Gigerenzer & Todd, 1999; Bowers & Davis, 2012). Indeed, there seems at first glance to be evidence that directly contradicts this assumption (Fu & Gray, 2004, 2006). In what follows we give our view on some of the controversies.

Optimality versus suboptimality: The semantic issue.   One well known HCI phenomenon is that people appear to persist in using apparently inefficient procedures in interactive tasks (Carroll & Rosson, 1987; Bhavnani & John, 2000; Fu & Gray, 2004), although see Charman & Howes (2003). They do so in the presence of demonstrably more efficient procedures. One possible conclusion is that people are suboptimal and therefore an optimisation-based framework like Adaptive Interaction must be unpromising. For example, Bhavnani & John (2000) observed that users of a drawing package usually fail to discover efficient strategies for grouping, aggregating, and manipulating graphic objects, and suggested that such strategies should be explicitly taught during training, alongside the more traditional instruction in the component operations provided by the device. Evidence reported by Fu & Gray (2004) suggests that the preferred, less efficient procedures, have two characteristics: (i) the preferred procedure is well practised and can be deployed for a variety of task environments, and (ii) the preferred procedure has a structure that gives step-by-step feedback on progress, or in other words, it is more interactive. According to Fu & Gray (2004) these users are suboptimal because they are biased to use more interactive and general procedures. This bias towards procedures that are globally efficient leads people to exhibit stable local suboptimalities. However, any conclusion of suboptimality is relative to a particular theory of utility, and local suboptimalities may well be globally optimal. The challenge is to find a theory of utility, context (global or local), and mechanism that explains the observed behaviour. Ultimately suboptimal adaptation to conditions X must be explained. The character of the explanation will, we anticipate, have the form, people were not adapting to X but to Y.

Why suboptimality is not an explanation.   Some authors go further than attempting to identify behaviours that are suboptimal given a particular theoretical standpoint concerning utility, environment, and mechanisms, to state that people are suboptimal without precisely stating the conditions, appearing to accept suboptimality in-and-of-itself as a sufficient *explanation*. Some even go as far as to claim that people are irrational. However, according to the Adaptive Interaction framework if people use a strategy that is suboptimal with respect to a particular theory, then the choice of that strategy is unexplained by that theory. Such a finding carries no implications for whether the choice of the strategy will be optimal with respect to some other, as yet unspecified, theory. It is that new theory, once it is formed, that will provide the explanation, not the previous identification of a suboptimality with respect to what is arguably a failed theory.

Here it is worth noting that a different use of the word suboptimal, is to refer to the incontrovertible fact that *all* human choice is suboptimal with respect to an unbounded machine. While it is possible to theorise about such machines and their mathematical properties, they do not exist within the physical universe and it is not therefore surprising that people are suboptimal with respect to them. When a theorist takes cognitive mechanisms into account in determining an optimal strategy, that strategy is likely to be suboptimal in an imaginary world with unbounded cognition; which is exactly the point of the requirement to identify cognitive mechanisms in the Adaptive Interaction framework.

The heuristic value of the Adaptive Interaction framework.   One argument for assuming optimality is, it seems to us, heuristic—the optimality assumption uncovers scientific problems that other approaches tend to sweep under the table with descriptions that masquerade as explanations.

Imagine that you verify empirically that a person uses strategy P to perform some task. And that you can identify strategy Q to perform the task that seems "better," i.e., has higher utility in what you assume to be the person's utility space.

What answer is a satisfactory answer to the question—why doesn't the agent do Q?
We can only conceive of the following:

1. The utility of Q is actually lower, because it has costs that the agent does care about—i.e., the initial model of utility under which $Q > P$ was wrong.

2. Q can't be realised by the agent's machinery.

3. Q can't be learned given the agent's machinery.

4. Q can't be learned given the agent's experience.

What would opponents of optimisation-based approaches say? It seems to us that all they can say is that Q is completely irrelevant, because the mind is not equipped or bothered to find better solutions to its problems, rather is content to 'satisfice' or rest with 'good enough' solutions. In which case, aren't they merely blocking an opportunity to learn something about the agent or the agent's utility via the specification of Q?

Perhaps the good-enough notion can be raised above mere description towards explanation, if one takes it to mean that the utility curve flattens to an asymptotic region of indifference. But this still leaves the question of where and why in the gain-curve such a flattening occurs, which seems worth addressing (and indeed, just such concerns are an important component of prospect theory's approach to economic decision making (Kahneman & Tversky, 1979)).

Short versus long-term optimisation.   One common theme emerges in our discussion of memory and planning. Many of the phenomena appear to arise, we have argued, because users try to optimise immediate performance, in terms of efficiency. In many situations (though not all), this will be at the expense of learning, as indexed by longer term performance.

The idea that performance and learning might often be in competition, so that optimising short-term performance will be to the detriment of long-term learning may seem strange, especially from the point of view of theories of skill acquisition which have focussed on those learning processes, such as procedural chunking, which are an automatic by-product of performance. Nevertheless, a classic review of training (Schmidt & Bjork, 1992) stressed exactly this competition. Schmidt and Bjork showed that both in motor skill and cognitive skill, training methods that optimised immediate performance of a skill would often lead to poor longer-term retention of the skill and poor transfer to the real (non-training) situation. To be effective in the longer-term, training regimes should introduce difficulties for the learner that encourage them to practise the problems they will face in the transfer situation. These effective regimes are likely to produce worse performance during training than other regimes which provide so much support that real problems are not encountered.

From this perspective, it seems unsurprising that, left to manage their own learning and performance, people act in a way that is suboptimal in the longer term. The very attempt to optimise the efficiency of immediate task performance often tends to work against learning. (This dilemma is a fine-grained, specific component of Carroll & Rosson's (1987) "paradox of the active user," i.e., the idea that users of computer systems are so consumed with immediate productivity goals that they are not motivated to take time out to learn better ways of accomplishing their tasks.)

An important design challenge is to develop user interfaces and learning experience that help users better manage the competition between short-term and longer-term performance. It may seem unlikely, as it did to O'Hara & Payne (1998), that increasing the cost of primitive interactions would be a very useful design strategy, except perhaps in training interfaces, or in interfaces to safety-critical applications. With respect to training, Cockburn et al. (2007) explored just such a design intervention in the case of interfaces that rely on spatial memory, in particular keypad layouts and gesture shapes. Their design idea was to cover screen support for the relevant spatial information with 'frost' that the user could 'wipe away' if they required external support.

Fortunately, Gray et al. (2000) and Gray & Fu (2001) have shown that very small changes to the cost structure of interfaces can reliably shift users' strategies—"Milliseconds matter", as Gray puts it. This is at least suggestive that design might fruitfully manipulate the microstructure of interfaces so as to encourage behaviours that are beneficial in the longer term as well as adaptive for immediate performance. One example of such an intervention was explored by Duggan & Payne (2001). They studied people learning the interactive procedures required to program a VCR, with the critical manipulation being the number of steps learners would keep in mind before executing the steps during practice. Better long-term retention of the procedure was observed when learners were encouraged to hold several steps in mind. Further, this effective learning strategy could be readily encouraged by adding a small interactive cost to the consultation of the full procedure.

11.2   IMPLICATIONS FOR HCI INVESTIGATIONS

The Adaptive Interaction framework provides a way to understand the behaviour of users of technology in terms of the strategic choices they make, so as to maximise utility. In exploring these issues across a range of HCI phenomena we have, of course, drawn insight and inspiration from a wide range of empirical investigations. Not all of these investigations had the framework at their heart, but nevertheless exposed important aspects of human interaction with technology, in our judgment. But in fact, the framework has lessons for the kinds of investigation that are most likely to encourage understanding of HCI and our intention in this subsection is to explore these lessons and relate them to contemporary debates about the criteria by which HCI research should be evaluated.

We are especially interested in experimental studies (although not wishing to disregard observation per se), because we believe that the manipulation of independent variables and the measurement of the effects on behaviour hold out the most promise for understanding why people behave in the way they do. It seems to us that laboratory experiments are undervalued in some HCI circles, and that this is for reasons which, while not false, are exaggerated by critics.

One difficult problem with experimentation (although this is shared to some extent among any attempts to understand *why* people behave in the way they do) is understanding utility for experimental participants. What currency are participants trying to maximise?

A standard approach in HCI experimentation is to assume that aspects of efficiency matter to participants (as they often do to designers), but to not fully appreciate that aspects of efficiency may be traded off, one against the other. Thus, it is a standard practice in experimental work to ask participants to complete tasks "as quickly and accurately as possible" even though such an instruction is logically inconsistent. For many purposes this may not matter so much, as experimental conditions can be compared on both dependent measures, and effects on one in the absence of the other can still be meaningful.

Even if one is concerned with optimality analyses it is possible to make some headway without constraining individual speed accuracy trade-offs. One might test whether behaviours are "Pareto optimal" in that a gain in one currency (say speed) could not be achieved without a decrement in another (say accuracy). See for example Figure 4 in Brumby et al. (2007). But in general an investigator might well care about the way individuals trade currencies, and this can be investigated by manipulating the relative importance of currencies instructionally, to plot a trade-off curve for each individual, or by fixing a combined utility score which specifies and communicates to participants the relative value of the different criteria (e.g., by specifying a time cost for each error). Such considerations are standard in some arenas of human performance psychology, but relatively rare in HCI work, to our knowledge.

Alongside speed-accuracy trade-off, another common kind of trade-off in certain tasks is between hits and false alarms in classification tasks, as analysed by Signal Detection Theory. It is never enough to measure "hit rate" as a performance measure in such tasks, as a perfect hit rate can be accomplished by responding positively to all stimuli. This elementary methodological stricture is ignored in some HCI research.

Another lesson that our framework holds for experimental work is that performance, however measured, will be a function of ecology or at least its experience (very often what is manipulated in an HCI experiment), cognitive architecture (presumed invariant), and, crucially, strategy. This means that straightforward comparisons of two technologies to perform a task are never straightforward, and can only be understood if the strategy space is understood. It is quite possible that one technology will seem to be better for performing a task than another just because the users' initial strategy selection is a better fit for that technology. We assume that adaptive learning will eventually allow users to discover the best strategy for each technology, but a relatively short-lasting experiment may not allow the learning opportunities required for this adaptation to emerge.

Finally, we wish to comment on the thorny issue of "ecological validity" which is controversial in HCI and beyond. First, in light of the tutorial functions of this lecture it is worth noting that the term itself is ambiguous. It was initially coined by Brunswik (1955) to label an experimental approach that attempts to be representative of real world tasks by sampling across such task materials and task contexts (as well as across experimental participants). However, it is widely assumed to be related to (and often confused with) "external validity" which is the validity of generalisations from a particular study to other situations. Because of this assumption, ecological validity can be unwisely used to summarily dismiss the relevance of experimental studies for HCI and to prefer "in the wild" studies in some particular pre-existing context. Of course, the issues here are by no means new, and similar debates have been had, e.g., in social psychology, with different conclusions holding sway. Defenders of artificial experiments in social psychology (e.g., Berkowitz & Donnerstein, 1982) have pointed out that representative experimental designs may be important for establishing population estimates, but that experiments are not typically conducted for this purpose. Instead, experiments are designed to test causal hypotheses about the inter-relation of variables (in our case, hypotheses about the relation between ecology, strategy, utility, and behaviour). For these purposes, whether laboratory results generalise to other situations is itself an empirical question. Furthermore, where varieties of this question have been subject to test, the results support an optimistic conclusion (Berkowitz & Donnerstein, 1982).

Inevitably, generalising from experimental results entails an inductive risk. But so does generalising from one real-world context to another. Just because "in the wild" studies take place in a rich context it does not mean that the role of that context is necessarily understood, or the problems of generalisation to another context are any less problematic.

Of course, studies in the wild can be invaluable for identifying types of behaviour or tasks that people adopt. Consider a recent article by Y. Rogers (2011), and see also Marshall et al. (2011), which directly contrasts lab studies with wild studies. Rogers describes her own work on collaboration of teams around tabletop computers. She mentions laboratory studies which gave such teams collaborative tasks and tracked the effects of various design parameters on behaviour. But then she reports a wild study, placing the same tabletop in a tourist agency and noting that groups tend not to gather around it, but rather approach it one at a time. Rogers regards this observation as "contrary to our findings in the lab." But surely it is instead contrary to the assumptions made in the laboratory work—although of course it remains perfectly possible, it seems to us, that there exist other real world situations where people would indeed gather in collaborative groups around a tabletop. The quite narrow lesson from this "wild/lab mismatch," it seems to us, is that some laboratory tasks will not speak to some real world situations. Nevertheless, it should not be lost that the in the wild study surely has played an important role in exposing the existence of an activity or task that it is worthwhile to understand (we could call it serial use of an information resource by a group). But surely a good programme of research to understand that task may involve experimental laboratory work in which the task is, to some degree, modelled.

11.3   CONCLUSION

In our view, the neglect of utility maximising approaches in Human Factors and Human-Computer Interaction is to be regretted. We would argue that greater attention to work by Swets et al. (1961) on Signal Detection Theory, by Baron & Kleinman (1969) on optimal control under processing constraints, by Sorkin & Woods (1985) on collaborative SDT, by Dessouky et al. (1995) on optimal scheduling, by Erev & Gopher (1999) on cognitive game theory as well as others, over the 30 years since Card et al. (1983)'s foundation of the field, would have gone a substantial way to answering the need for theory in HCI. Perhaps, if this neglect can be reversed, then confusion about the role and importance of the influence of context on behaviour, which some use to deny the prospect of any scientific approach, can be overcome.

This argument may be easier to carry from a scientific than from a design-oriented perspective. We are interested in understanding how people interact with technologies as an intellectual problem, not just because we feel such an understanding has design implications. We recognise that there are considerable challenges in translating understanding into design implications, but believe that the full benefits of deep understandings, for design and for other important issues like education and policy, should not be second-guessed.

We hope that by returning attention to the extraordinarily adaptive, but nonetheless bounded, capacity of the human mind, genuinely predictive theories of what people *choose* to do with technology can be used to organise HCI research. If interaction can be understood in terms of the joint constraints imposed by utility, mechanism, and ecology, then HCI design can be underpinned by a relevant and useful empirical and theoretical program.

References

Adamczyk, P. D., & Bailey, B. P. (2004). If not now, when?: the effects of interruption at different moments within task execution. In *Proceedings of the sigchi conference on human factors in computing systems* (pp. 271–278). DOI: 10.1145/985692.985727 29

Allport, D. A., Styles, E. A., & Hsieh, S. (1994). Shifting intentional set: Exploring the dynamic control of tasks. 24

Altmann, E. M., & Trafton, J. G. (2002). Memory for goals: an activation-based model. *Cognitive Science*, *26*(1), 39–83. DOI: 10.1207/s15516709cog2601_2 25

Anderson, J. R. (1990). *The Adaptive Character of Thought.* Lawrence Erlbaum. 7

Anderson, J. R., Bothell, D., Byrne, M. D., Douglass, S., Lebiere, C., & Qin, Y. (2004). An integrated theory of the mind. *Psychological Review*, *111*(4), 1036–60. DOI: 10.1037/0033-295X.111.4.1036 9, 42

Ariely, D. (2009). *Predictably Irrational, Revised and Expanded Edition: The Hidden Forces that Shape our Decisions.* Harper. 11

Arora, A., González, V. M., & Payne, S. J. (2011). The Social Nature of Work Fragmentation: Revisiting Informal Workplace Communication. *Ergonomics Open Journal*, *4*, 23–27. DOI: 10.2174/1875934301104010023 23

Asch, S. E. (1951). Effects of group pressure upon the modification and distortion of judgments. 20

Axelrod, R. M. (1997). *The complexity of cooperation: Agent-based models of competition and collabora- tion.* Princeton Univ Pr. 72

Baddeley, A. D., & Hitch, G. J. (1974). Working memory. *The psychology of learning and motivation*, *8*, 47–89. DOI: 10.1016/S0079-7421(08)60452-1 24

Bahrami, B., Olsen, K., Latham, P. E., Roepstorff, A., Rees, G., & Frith, C. D. (2010). Optimally Interacting Minds. *Science*, *329*(5995), 1081–1085. DOI: 10.1126/science.1185718 19

Ballard, D. H., Hayhoe, M. M., Pook, P. K., & Rao, R. P. N. (1997). Deictic codes for the embodiment of cognition. *Behavioral and Brain Sciences*, *20*(04), 723–742. DOI: 10.1017/S0140525X97001611 3

84 REFERENCES

Baron, S., & Kleinman, D. L. (1969). The human as an optimal controller and information processor. *Man-Machine Systems, IEEE Transactions on, 10*(1), 9–17. DOI: 10.1109/TMMS.1969.299875 5, 7, 81

Bellotti, V., Ducheneaut, N., Howard, M., & Smith, I. (2003). Taking email to task: the design and evaluation of a task management centered email tool. In *Proceedings of the sigchi conference on human factors in computing systems* (pp. 345–352). DOI: 10.1145/642611.642672 63

Bentham, J. (1789). *An introduction to the principles of morals and legislation.* 4

Berkowitz, L., & Donnerstein, E. (1982). External validity is more than skin deep: Some answers to criticisms of laboratory experiments. *American psychologist, 37*(3), 245. DOI: 10.1037/0003-066X.37.3.245 80

Bhavnani, S. K., & John, B. E. (2000). The strategic use of complex computer systems. *Human–Computer Interaction, 15*(2-3), 107–137. DOI: 10.1207/S15327051HCI1523_3 64, 66, 76

Binder, J., Howes, A., & Smart, D. (2012). Harmony and tension on social network sites: side-effects of increasing online interconnectivity. *Information, Communication and Society.* DOI: 10.1080/1369118X.2011.648949 4

Binder, J., Howes, A., & Sutcliffe, A. (2009). The problem of conflicting social spheres: effects of network structure on experienced tension in social network sites. In *Proceedings of the 27th international conference on human factors in computing systems* (pp. 965–974). DOI: 10.1145/1518701.1518849 4

Bolton, G., Katok, E., & Ockenfels, A. (2004). How effective are electronic reputation mechanisms? An experimental investigation. *Management Science, 50*(11), 1587–1602. DOI: 10.1287/mnsc.1030.0199 69, 71, 74

Bowers, J. S., & Davis, C. J. (2012). Bayesian just-so stories in psychology and neuroscience. *Psychological bulletin, 138*(3), 389. DOI: 10.1037/a0026450 11, 76

Boyd, R., & Richerson, P. J. (1988). The evolution of reciprocity in sizable groups. *Journal of Theoretical Biology, 132*(3), 337–356. DOI: 10.1016/S0022-5193(88)80219-4 72

Brumby, D. P., Salvucci, D. D., & Howes, A. (2009). Focus on driving: How cognitive constraints shape the adaptation of strategy when dialing while driving. In *Proceedings of the 27th international conference on human factors in computing systems* (pp. 1629–1638). DOI: 10.1145/1518701.1518950 10, 24, 26

Brumby, D. P., Salvucci, D. D., Mankowski, W., & Howes, A. (2007). A cognitive constraint model of the effects of portable music-player use on driver performance. *Proceedings of the Human Factors and Ergonomics Society Annual Meeting, 51*(24), 1531–1535. DOI: 10.1177/154193120705102404 10, 26, 79

Bruner, J. S. (1961). The act of discovery. *Harvard educational review*. 4

Brunswik, E. (1955). Representative design and probabilistic theory in a functional psychology. *Psychological Review*, *62*(3), 193. DOI: 10.1037/h0047470 80

Buchanan, G., & Loizides, F. (2007). Investigating document triage on paper and electronic media. *Research and Advanced Technology for Digital Libraries*, 416–427. DOI: 10.1007/978-3-540-74851-9_35 52

Buchanan, G., & Owen, T. (2008). Improving skim reading for document triage. In *Proceedings of the second international symposium on information interaction in context* (pp. 83–88). DOI: 10.1145/1414694.1414714 52

Card, S. K., Moran, T. P., & Newell, A. (1983). The Psychology of Human-Computer Interaction Lawrence Erlbaum Associates. *Hillsdale, NJ*. 9, 31, 37, 81

Carroll, J. M., & Rosson, M. B. (1987). *Paradox of the active user*. The MIT Press. 76, 78

Carver, R. P. (1984). Rauding theory predictions of amount comprehended under different purposes and speed reading conditions. *Reading Research Quarterly*, 205–218. DOI: 10.2307/747363 52

Charman, S. C., & Howes, A. (2003). The adaptive user: an investigation into the cognitive and task constraints on the generation of new methods. *Journal of experimental psychology. Applied*, *9*(4), 236–48. DOI: 10.1037/1076-898X.9.4.236 66, 76

Charnov, E. L. (1976). Optimal foraging, the marginal value theorem. *Theoretical population biology*, *9*(2), 129–136. DOI: 10.1016/0040-5809(76)90040-X 8, 27

Chase, V., Hertwig, R., & Gigerenzer, G. (1998). Visions of rationality? *Trends in cognitive sciences*, *2*(6), 206–214. DOI: 10.1016/S1364-6613(98)01179-6 11, 46

Chi, C. F., & Drury, C. G. (1998). Do people choose an optimal response criterion in an inspection task? *IIE transactions*, *30*(3), 257–266. DOI: 10.1023/A:1007482604749 16

Clarkson, E., Clawson, J., Lyons, K., & Starner, T. (2005). An empirical study of typing rates on mini-QWERTY keyboards. In *Chi'05 extended abstracts on human factors in computing systems* (pp. 1288–1291). DOI: 10.1145/1056808.1056898 40

Cockburn, A., Kristensson, P. O., Alexander, J., & Zhai, S. (2007). Hard lessons: effort-inducing interfaces benefit spatial learning. In *Proceedings of the sigchi conference on human factors in computing systems* (pp. 1571–1580). DOI: 10.1145/1240624.1240863 78

Cockburn, A., Savage, J., & Wallace, A. (2005). Tuning and testing scrolling interfaces that automatically zoom. In *Proceedings of the sigchi conference on human factors in computing systems* (pp. 71–80). DOI: 10.1145/1054972.1054983 52

Coover, J. E. (1923). A method of teaching typewriting based on a psychological analysis of expert typing. *National Educational Association`Addresses and Proceedings*, *61*, 561–567. 40

Dellarocas, C. (2003). The digitization of word of mouth: Promise and challenges of online feedback mechanisms. *Management science*, 1407–1424. DOI: 10.1287/mnsc.49.10.1407.17308 45

Dessouky, M. I., Moray, N., & Kijowski, B. (1995). Taxonomy of scheduling systems as a basis for the study of strategic behavior. *Human Factors: The Journal of the Human Factors and Ergonomics Society*, *37*(3), 443–472. DOI: 10.1518/001872095779049282 7, 24, 25, 29, 81

Dix, A., Howes, A., & Payne, S. J. (2003). Post-web cognition: evolving knowledge strategies for global information environments. *International journal of Web engineering and technology*, *1*(1), 112–126. DOI: 10.1504/IJWET.2003.003323 3, 61

Dourish, P. (2004). What we talk about when we talk about context. *Personal and ubiquitous computing*, *8*(1), 19–30. DOI: 10.1007/s00779-003-0253-8 1, 2, 3, 4

Draper, S. W. (1986). Display managers as the basis for user machine communication. In D. A. Norman & S. W. Draper (Eds.), *User centred system design*. Hillsdale, NJ: Lawrence Erlbaum Associates. 64

Duggan, G. B., Banbury, S., Howes, A., Patrick, J., & Waldron, S. M. (2004). Too much, too little or just right: Designing data fusion for situation awareness. *Proceedings of the Human Factors and Ergonomics Society Annual Meeting*, *48*(3), 528–532. DOI: 10.1177/154193120404800354 10

Duggan, G. B., & Payne, S. J. (2001). Interleaving reading and acting while following procedural instructions. *Journal of Experimental Psychology: Applied*, *7*(4), 10. DOI: 10.1037/1076-898X.7.4.297 78

Duggan, G. B., & Payne, S. J. (2008). Knowledge in the head and on the web: using topic expertise to aid search. In *Proceedings of the twenty-sixth annual sigchi conference on human factors in computing systems* (pp. 39–48). DOI: 10.1145/1357054.1357062 62

Duggan, G. B., & Payne, S. J. (2009). Text skimming: The process and effectiveness of foraging through text under time pressure. *Journal of Experimental Psychology: Applied; Journal of Experimental Psychology: Applied*, *15*(3), 228. DOI: 10.1037/a0016995 ix, 51, 52, 56, 58, 59

Duggan, G. B., & Payne, S. J. (2011). Skim reading by satisficing: evidence from eye tracking. In *Proceedings of the 2011 annual conference on human factors in computing systems* (pp. 1141–1150). DOI: 10.1145/1978942.1979114 ix, 52, 56, 58, 59

Dyson, M., & Haselgrove, M. (2000). The effects of reading speed and reading patterns on the understanding of text read from screen. *Journal of Research in Reading*, *23*(2), 210–223. DOI: 10.1111/1467-9817.00115 52

Dyson, M. C., & Haselgrove, M. (2001). The influence of reading speed and line length on the effectiveness of reading from screen. *International Journal of Human-Computer Studies*, *54*(4), 585–612. DOI: 10.1006/ijhc.2001.0458 52

Eng, K., Lewis, R. L., Tollinger, I., Chu, A., Howes, A., & Vera, A. (2006). Generating automated predictions of behavior strategically adapted to specific performance objectives. In *Proceedings of the sigchi conference on human factors in computing systems* (pp. 621–630). DOI: 10.1145/1124772.1124866 5, 10, 65

Erev, I., & Gopher, D. (1999). A cognitive game-theory analysis of attention strategies, ability, and incentives. In D. Gopher & A. Koriat (Eds.), *Attention and performance xviii - cognitive regulation of performance: Theory and application* (pp. 343–372). Cambridge, MA: MIT Press. 5, 7, 9, 11, 12, 16, 17, 18, 81

Erev, I., & Roth, A. E. (1998). Predicting how people play games: Reinforcement learning in experimental games with unique, mixed strategy equilibria. *American economic review*, 848–881. 8

Faisal, A. A., Selen, L. P. J., & Wolpert, D. M. (2008). Noise in the nervous system. *Nature Reviews Neuroscience*, *9*(4), 292–303. DOI: 10.1038/nrn2258 31, 32

Farmer, G., Janssen, C. P., & Brumby, D. P. (2011). How long have I got? Making optimal visit durations in a dual-task setting. In *Proceedings of the 33rd annual meeting of the cognitive science society*. 24, 26

Fehr, E., Kremhelmer, S., & Schmidt, K. M. (2008). Fairness and the Optimal Allocation of Ownership Rights*. *The Economic Journal*, *118*(531), 1262–1284. DOI: 10.1111/j.1468-0297.2008.02169.x 4, 5

Feigh, K. M., Dorneich, M. C., & Hayes, C. C. (2012). Toward a Characterization of Adaptive Systems: A Framework for Researchers and System Designers. *Human Factors: The Journal of the Human Factors and Ergonomics Society*. DOI: 10.1177/0018720812443983 29

Fitts, P. M. (1954). The information capacity of the human motor system in controlling the amplitude of movement. *Journal of experimental psychology*, *47*(6), 381. DOI: 10.1037/h0055392 31, 37

Foltz, P. W. (1996). Comprehension, coherence, and strategies in hypertext and linear text. *Hypertext and cognition*, 109–136. 55

Fu, W.-T., & Gray, W. D. (2004). Resolving the paradox of the active user: stable suboptimal performance in interactive tasks. *Cognitive Science*, *28*, 901–935. DOI: 10.1207/s15516709cog2806_2 64, 65, 76

Fu, W.-T., & Gray, W. D. (2006). Suboptimal tradeoffs in information seeking. *Cognitive Psychology*, *52*(3), 195–242. DOI: 10.1016/j.cogpsych.2005.08.002 11, 64, 66, 76

Galton, F. (1907). Vox populi. *Nature*, *75*, 450–451. 20

Garrod, S., & Doherty, G. (1994). Conversation, co-ordination and convention: An empirical investigation of how groups establish linguistic conventions. *Cognition*, *53*(3), 181–215. DOI: 10.1016/0010-0277(94)90048-5 4

Gigerenzer, G., & Todd, P. M. (1999). Fast and frugal heuristics: The adaptive toolbox. 76

Goeree, J. K., & Holt, C. A. (2001). Ten little treasures of game theory and ten intuitive contradictions. *American Economic Review*, 1402–1422. DOI: 10.1257/aer.91.5.1402 72

González, V. M., & Mark, G. (2005). Managing currents of work: multi-tasking among multiple collaborations. In *Ecscw 2005* (pp. 143–162). DOI: 10.1007/1-4020-4023-7_8 23, 28

Gray, W. D., & Fu, W.-T. (2001). Ignoring perfect knowledge in-the-world for imperfect knowledge in-the-head: Implications of rational analysis for interface design. *CHI Letters*, *3*(3), 112–119. DOI: 10.1145/365024.365061 3, 64, 78

Gray, W. D., & Fu, W.-T. (2004). Soft constraints in interactive behavior : the case of ignoring perfect knowledge in-the-world for imperfect knowledge in-the-head. *Cognitive Science*, *28*, 359–382. DOI: 10.1207/s15516709cog2803_3 7

Gray, W. D., Schoelles, M. J., & Fu, W.-T. (2000). Modeling a Continuous Dynamic Task. *Human Factors*. 44, 65, 78

Gray, W. D., Sims, C. R., Fu, W.-T., & Schoelles, M. J. (2006). The soft constraints hypothesis: a rational analysis approach to resource allocation for interactive behavior. *Psychological review*, *113*(3), 461–82. DOI: 10.1037/0033-295X.113.3.461 3, 7

Green, D. M., & Swets, J. A. (1966). *Signal detection theory and psychophysics* (Vol. 1974). Wiley New York. 12

Green, R. F. (1984). Stopping rules for optimal foragers. *American Naturalist*, 30–43. DOI: 10.1086/284184 28

Guiard, Y., Olafsdottir, H. B., & Perrault, S. T. (2011). Fitt's law as an explicit time/error trade-off. In *Proceedings of the 2011 annual conference on human factors in computing systems* (pp. 1619–1628). DOI: 10.1145/1978942.1979179 31, 36

Hagerty, M. R., & Aaker, D. A. (1984). A normative model of consumer information processing. *Marketing Science*, *3*(3), 227–246. DOI: 10.1287/mksc.3.3.227 46

Harris, C. M., & Wolpert, D. M. (2006). The main sequence of saccades optimizes speed-accuracy trade-off. *Biological cybernetics*, *95*(1), 21–29. DOI: 10.1007/s00422-006-0064-x 31

Harvey, N., & Bolger, F. (2001). Collecting information: Optimizing outcomes, screening options, or facilitating discrimination? *The Quarterly Journal of Experimental Psychology: Section A*, *54*(1), 269–301. DOI: 10.1080/02724980042000110 47

Hays, R. B. (1985). A longitudinal study of friendship development. *Journal of Personality and Social Psychology*, *48*(4), 909. DOI: 10.1037/0022-3514.48.4.909 72

Heath, C., & Luff, P. (1992). Collaboration and controlCrisis management and multimedia technology in London Underground Line Control Rooms. *Computer Supported Cooperative Work (CSCW)*, *1*(1), 69–94. DOI: 10.1007/BF00752451 3, 4

Hockey, G. R. J., Wastell, D. G., & Sauer, J. (1998). Effects of sleep deprivation and user interface on complex performance: a multilevel analysis of compensatory control. *Human Factors: The Journal of the Human Factors and Ergonomics Society*, *40*(2), 233–253. DOI: 10.1518/001872098779480479 26

Hollan, J., Hutchins, E., & Kirsh, D. (2000). Distributed Cognition : Toward a New Foundation for Human-Computer Interaction Research. , *7*(2), 174 –196. DOI: 10.1145/353485.353487 3, 63

Howes, A. (1993). Recognition-based Problem Solving. In *Fifteenth annual conference of the cognitive science society* (pp. 551–556). 3, 61

Howes, A. (1994). A model of the acquisition of menu knowledge by exploration. In *Proceedings of the sigchi conference on human factors in computing systems: celebrating interdependence* (pp. 445–451). DOI: 10.1145/191666.191820 3

Howes, A., Lewis, R. L., & Vera, A. (2009). Rational adaptation under task and processing constraints: implications for testing theories of cognition and action. *Psychological Review*, *116*(4), 717–751. DOI: 10.1037/a0017187 ix, 7, 9, 11, 12, 36, 39, 41, 42, 43, 44, 64, 75

Howes, A., Lewis, R. L., Vera, A., & Richardson, J. (2005). Information-Requirements Grammar: A theory of the structure of competence for interaction. *Proceedings of the 27th Annual Meeting of the Cognitive Science Society*, 977–983. 10, 42, 44, 65

Howes, A., & Payne, S. J. (1990). Display-based competence: towards user models for menu-driven interfaces. *International Journal of Man-Machine Studies*, *33*(6), 637–655. DOI: 10.1016/S0020-7373(05)80067-7 3, 61

Howes, A., Payne, S. J., & Richardson, J. (2002). An instance-based model of the effect of previous choices on the control of interactive search. *Proceedings of the 24th annual meeting of the Cognitive Science Society*, 476–481. 67

Howes, A., Vera, A., Lewis, R. L., & McCurdy, M. (2004). Cognitive constraint modeling: A formal approach to supporting reasoning about behavior. *Proc. Cognitive Science Society*, 595–600. 5, 9, 10, 42, 44, 65

Howes, A., & Young, R. M. (1996). Learning consistent, interactive, and meaningful task-action mappings: A computational model. *Cognitive Science*, *20*(3), 301–356. DOI: 10.1207/s15516709cog2003_1 61

Hutchins, E. (2010). Cognitive ecology. *Topics in Cognitive Science*, *2*(4), 705–715. DOI: 10.1111/j.1756-8765.2010.01089.x 3

Hutchins, E., & Lintern, G. (1995). *Cognition in the Wild* (Vol. 262082314). MIT press Cambridge, MA. 4, 63

Jagacinski, R. J., & Flach, J. (2003). *Control theory for humans: Quantitative approaches to modeling performance*. CRC. 31, 36

Janssen, C. P., Brumby, D. P., Dowell, J., Chater, N., & Howes, A. (2011). Identifying optimum performance trade-offs using a cognitively bounded rational analysis model of discretionary task interleaving. *Topics in Cognitive Science*, *3*(1), 123–139. DOI: 10.1111/j.1756-8765.2010.01125.x 5, 10, 24, 26

John, B. E., & Newell, A. (1989). Cumulating the science of HCI: From SR compatibility to transcription typing. In *Acm sigchi bulletin* (Vol. 20, pp. 109–114). DOI: 10.1145/67450.67472 39

Jones, K. E., Hamilton, A. F. C., & Wolpert, D. M. (2002). Sources of signal-dependent noise during isometric force production. *Journal of neurophysiology*, *88*(3), 1533–1544. 34

Kahneman, D., & Tversky, A. (1979). Prospect theory: An analysis of decision under risk. *Econometrica: Journal of the Econometric Society*, 263–291. DOI: 10.2307/1914185 4, 5, 77

Kiwan, D., Ahmed, A., & Pollitt, A. (2000). The effects of time-induced stress on making inferences in text comprehension. In *European conference on educational research, edinburgh.* 52

Krebs, J. R., Kacelnik, A., & Taylor, P. (1978). Test of optimal sampling by foraging great tits. *Nature*, *275*(5675), 27–31. DOI: 10.1038/275027a0 54

Kristensson, P. O. (2009). Five challenges for intelligent text entry methods. *AI Magazine*, *30*(4), 85. 39

Kubovy, M., Rapoport, A., & Tversky, A. (1971). Deterministic vs probabilistic strategies in detection. *Attention, Perception, & Psychophysics*, *9*(5), 427–429. DOI: 10.3758/BF03210245 16

Lave, J. (1988). *Cognition in practice: Mind, mathematics and culture in everyday life*. Cambridge University Press. DOI: 10.1017/CBO9780511609268 3, 4

Lee, J., Park, D. H., & Han, I. (2008). The effect of negative online consumer reviews on product attitude: An information processing view. *Electronic Commerce Research and Applications, 7*(3), 341–352. DOI: 10.1016/j.elerap.2007.05.004 48

Lelis, S., & Howes, A. (2008). A Bayesian Model of How People Search Online Consumer Reviews. *Proc. CogSci 2008*, 553–558. ix, 10, 45, 49

Lelis, S., & Howes, A. (2011). Informing decisions: how people use online rating information to make choices. In *Proceedings of the 2011 annual conference on human factors in computing systems* (pp. 2285–2294). DOI: 10.1145/1978942.1979278 ix, 10, 46, 47, 48, 49

Lewis, R. L., Vera, A. H., & Howes, A. H. (2004). A constraint-based approach to understanding the composition of skill. *Proceedings of the Sixth International Conference on Cognitive Modeling*, 148–153. 10

Liu, Z. (2005). Reading behavior in the digital environment: Changes in reading behavior over the past ten years. *Journal of Documentation, 61*(6), 700–712. DOI: 10.1108/00220410510632040 51

Lohse, G., & Johnson, E. (1996). A Comparison of Two Process Tracing Methods for Choice Tasks. *Organizational Behavior and Human Decision Processes, 68*(1), 28–43. DOI: 10.1006/obhd.1996.0087 49

Lorenz, J., Rauhut, H., Schweitzer, F., & Helbing, D. (2011). How social influence can undermine the wisdom of crowd effect. *Proceedings of the National Academy of Sciences, 108*(22), 9020–9025. DOI: 10.1073/pnas.1008636108 20

Lynch, J. G., & Ariely, D. (2000). Wine Online: Search Costs Affect Competition on Price, Quality, and Distribution. *Marketing Science, 19*(1), 83–103. DOI: 10.1287/mksc.19.1.83.15183 48

MacKenzie, I. S. (1992). Fitts' law as a research and design tool in human-computer interaction. *Human-computer interaction, 7*(1), 91–139. DOI: 10.1207/s15327051hci0701_3 31, 37

MacKenzie, I. S., & Soukoreff, R. W. (2002). Text entry for mobile computing: Models and methods, theory and practice. *Human–Computer Interaction, 17*(2-3), 147–198. DOI: 10.1207/S15327051HCI172&3_2 40

MacLean, A., Young, R. M., Bellotti, V. M. E., & Moran, T. P. (1991). Questions, options, and criteria: Elements of design space analysis. *Human–computer interaction, 6*(3-4), 201–250. DOI: 10.1207/s15327051hci0603&4_2 12

Mailath, G. J., & Samuelson, L. (2006). *Repeated games and reputations: long-run relationships.* Oxford University Press, USA. DOI: 10.1093/acprof:oso/9780195300796.001.0001 72, 73

Malone, T. W., Yates, J., & Benjamin, R. I. (1987). Electronic markets and electronic hierarchies. *Communications of the ACM, 30*(6), 484–497. DOI: 10.1145/214762.214766 69

Maloney, L. T., & Mamassian, P. (2009). Bayesian decision theory as a model of human visual perception: testing Bayesian transfer. *Visual neuroscience*, *26*(1), 147–55. DOI: 10.1017/S0952523808080905 31, 32

Maloney, L. T., Trommershäuser, J., Landy, M. S., & Gray, W. (2007). Questions without words: A comparison between decision making under risk and movement planning under risk. *Integrated models of cognitive systems*, 297–313. DOI: 10.1093/acprof:oso/9780195189193.003.0021 32

Marcus, G. (2009). *Kluge: The haphazard evolution of the human mind.* Mariner Books. 11

Mark, G., Gonzalez, V. M., & Harris, J. (2005). No task left behind?: examining the nature of fragmented work. In *Proceedings of the sigchi conference on human factors in computing systems* (pp. 321–330). DOI: 10.1145/1054972.1055017 23

Marshall, P., Morris, R., Rogers, Y., Kreitmayer, S., & Davies, M. (2011). Rethinking'multi-user': an in-the-wild study of how groups approach a walk-up-and-use tabletop interface. In *Proceedings of the 2011 annual conference on human factors in computing systems* (pp. 3033–3042). DOI: 10.1145/1978942.1979392 80

Masson, M. E. (1982a). Cognitive processes in skimming stories. *Journal of Experimental Psychology: Learning, Memory, and Cognition*, *8*(5), 400. DOI: 10.1037/0278-7393.8.5.400 51, 52

Masson, M. E. (1982b). A framework of cognitive and metacognitive determinants of reading skill. *Topics in Learning & Learning Disabilities; Topics in Learning & Learning Disabilities.* 51

Mayes, J., Draper, S., McGregor, A., & Oatley, K. (1988). Information flow in a user interface: The effect of experience and context on the recall of MacWrite screens. In *Conference of the british computer society human-computer interaction specialist group; manchester (uk).* (pp. 275–289). 63

McFarlane, D. C., & Latorella, K. A. (2002). The scope and importance of human interruption in human-computer interaction design. *Human-Computer Interaction*, *17*(1), 1–61. DOI: 10.1207/S15327051HCI1701_1 29

Metcalfe, J. (2002). Is study time allocated selectively to a region of proximal learning? *Journal of Experimental Psychology: General*, *131*(3), 349. DOI: 10.1037/0096-3445.131.3.349 54

Meyer, D., Abrams, R., Kornblum, S., Wright, C., & Smith, J. (1988). Optimality in human motor performance: Ideal control of rapid aimed movements. *Psychological Review*, *95*(3), 340–370. DOI: 10.1037/0033-295X.95.3.340 31, 36, 75

Meyer, D., & Kieras, D. (1997). A computational theory of executive cognitive processes and multiple-task performance: Part 1. Basic mechanisms. *Psychological Review*, *104*(1), 3. DOI: 10.1037/0033-295X.104.1.3 9, 42

Miles, G. E., Howes, A., & Davies, A. (2000). A framework for understanding human factors in web-based electronic commerce. *International Journal of Human-Computer Studies*, *52*(1), 131–163. DOI: 10.1006/ijhc.1999.0324 49

Milinski, M., & Wedekind, C. (1998). Working memory constrains human cooperation in the Prisoner's Dilemma. *Proceedings of the National Academy of Sciences*, *95*(23), 13755–13758. DOI: 10.1073/pnas.95.23.13755 73

Moray, N., Dessouky, M. I., Kijowski, B. A., & Adapathya, R. (1991). Strategic behavior, workload, and performance in task scheduling. *Human Factors: The Journal of the Human Factors and Ergonomics Society*, *33*(6), 607–629. DOI: 10.1177/001872089103300602 5, 25, 29

Morkes, J., & Nielsen, J. (1997). Concise, scannable, and objective: How to write for the Web. *Useit. com*. 51

Morton, J. (1967). A Singular Lack of Incidental Learning. *Nature*, *215*(5097), 203–204. DOI: 10.1038/215203a0 63

Nelson, J. D. (2008). Towards a rational theory of human information acquisition. *The probabilistic mind: Prospects for rational models of cognition*, 143–163. DOI: 10.1093/acprof:oso/9780199216093.003.0007 46

Neumann, J. von, & Morgenstern, O. (1947). Theory of games and economic behavior. *Princeton University, Princeton*. 4

Newell, A. (1990). *Unified theories of cognition*. Harvard Univ Press. 9

Norman, D. A. (1983). Design principles for Human-Computer Interaction. In *Proceedings of chi'83*. ACM. 5, 7

Norman, D. A., & Bobrow, D. G. (1979). Descriptions: An intermediate stage in memory retrieval. *Cognitive Psychology*, *11*(1), 107–123. DOI: 10.1016/0010-0285(79)90006-9 62

Nowak, M., & Sigmund, K. (1998). Evolution of indirect reciprocity by image scoring. *Nature*, *393*, 573–577. DOI: 10.1038/31225 73

Nowak, M., & Sigmund, K. (2005). Evolution of indirect reciprocity. *Nature*, *437*(7063), 1291–1298. DOI: 10.1038/nature04131 5, 73

O'Hara, K. P., & Payne, S. J. (1998). The effects of operator implementation cost on planfulness of problem solving and learning. *Cognitive psychology*, *35*(1), 34–70. DOI: 10.1006/cogp.1997.0676 3, 67, 78

O'Hara, K. P., & Payne, S. J. (1999). Planning and the user interface: The effects of lockout time and error recovery cost. *International Journal of Human-Computer Studies*, *50*(1), 41–59. DOI: 10.1006/ijhc.1998.0234 3, 67

Olson, G. M., & Olson, J. S. (2000). Distance matters. *Human-computer interaction, 15*(2), 139–178. DOI: 10.1207/S15327051HCI1523_4 4

Oviatt, S., DeAngeli, A., & Kuhn, K. (1997). Integration and synchronization of input modes during multimodal human-computer interaction. In *Referring phenomena in a multimedia context and their computational treatment* (pp. 1–13). DOI: 10.3115/1621585.1621587 39

Parhi, P., Karlson, A. K., & Bederson, B. B. (2006). Target size study for one-handed thumb use on small touchscreen devices. In *Proceedings of the 8th conference on human-computer interaction with mobile devices and services* (pp. 203–210). DOI: 10.1145/1152215.1152260 37

Payne, J. W. (1996, May). When Time Is Money: Decision Behavior under Opportunity-Cost Time Pressure. *Organizational Behavior and Human Decision Processes, 66*(2), 131–152. DOI: 10.1006/obhd.1996.0044 47

Payne, J. W., Bettman, J. R., & Johnson, E. J. (1988). Adaptive strategy selection in decision making. *Journal of Experimental Psychology: Learning, Memory and Cognition, 14*(3), 534–552. DOI: 10.1037/0278-7393.14.3.534 46, 47

Payne, S. J. (1991). Display-based action at the user interface. *International Journal of Man-Machine Studies, 35*(3), 275–289. DOI: 10.1016/S0020-7373(05)80129-4 61, 64

Payne, S. J. (1993). Understanding calendar use. *Human-Computer Interaction, 8*(2), 83–100. DOI: 10.1207/s15327051hci0802_1 63

Payne, S. J., Duggan, G., & Neth, H. (2007). Discretionary task interleaving: Heuristics for time allocation in cognitive foraging. *JOURNAL OF EXPERIMENTAL PSYCHOLOGY GENERAL, 136*(3), 370. DOI: 10.1037/0096-3445.136.3.370 ix, 23, 24, 26, 27, 28

Payne, S. J., Howes, A., & Reader, W. R. (2001). Adaptively distributing cognition: a decision-making perspective on human-computer interaction. *Behaviour & Information Technology, 20*(5), 339–346. DOI: 10.1080/01449290110078680 ix, 3, 7, 61, 63

Payne, S. J., Richardson, J., & Howes, A. (2000). Strategic use of familiarity in display-based problem solving. *Journal of Experimental Psychology: Learning, Memory, and Cognition, 26*(6), 1685. DOI: 10.1037/0278-7393.26.6.1685 61, 66

Pete, A., Pattipati, K. R., & Kleinman, D. L. (1993). Optimal team and individual decision rules in uncertain dichotomous situations. *Public Choice, 75*(3), 205–230. DOI: 10.1007/BF01119183 17

Phelps, S., Nevarez, G., & Howes, A. (2009). The effect of group size and frequency-of-encounter on the evolution of cooperation. In *Lncs, volume 5778, advances in artificial life: Darwin meets von neumann* (pp. 34–37). DOI: 10.1007/978-3-642-21314-4_5 72

Pirolli, P. (2007). *Information foraging theory: Adaptive interaction with information* (Vol. 2). Oxford University Press, USA. DOI: 10.1093/acprof:oso/9780195173321.001.0001 48

Pirolli, P., & Card, S. (1999). Information foraging. *Psychological Review, 106,* 643–675. DOI: 10.1037/0033-295X.106.4.643 7, 8, 46, 52, 54

Reader, W. R., & Payne, S. J. (2007). Allocating time across multiple texts: Sampling and satisficing. *Human–Computer Interaction, 22*(3), 263–298. DOI: 10.1080/07370020701493376 ix, 26, 51, 52, 53, 56, 57, 58

Roberts, G., & Sherratt, T. (1998a). Development of cooperative relationships through increasing investment. *Nature, 394*(6689), 175–179. DOI: 10.1038/28160 31

Roberts, G., & Sherratt, T. N. (1998b). Development of cooperative relationships through increasing investment. *Nature, 394*(6689), 175–179. DOI: 10.1038/28160 72

Rogers, R. D., & Monsell, S. (1995). Costs of a predictible switch between simple cognitive tasks. *Journal of experimental psychology: General, 124*(2), 207. DOI: 10.1037/0096-3445.124.2.207 24

Rogers, Y. (2011). Interaction design gone wild: striving for wild theory. *interactions, 18*(4), 58–62. DOI: 10.1145/1978822.1978834 1, 3, 80

Rogers, Y., & Brignull, H. (2003). Computational offloading: Supporting distributed team working through visually augmenting verbal communication. In *Proc. 25th annual conference of the cognitive science society (COGSCI'03).* 3

Roth, A. E., & Erev, I. (1995). Learning in extensive-form games: Experimental data and simple dynamic models in the intermediate term. *Games and economic behavior, 8*(1), 164–212. DOI: 10.1016/S0899-8256(05)80020-X 8

Rouet, J. F., Favart, M., Britt, M. A., & Perfetti, C. A. (1997). Studying and using multiple documents in history: Effects of discipline expertise. *Cognition and Instruction, 15*(1), 85–106. DOI: 10.1207/s1532690xci1501_3 53

Russell, S., & Subramanian, D. (1995). Provably bounded-optimal agents. *Journal of Artificial Intelligence Research, 2,* 575–609. 7

Salthouse, T. A. (1986). Perceptual , Cognitive , and Motoric Aspects of Transcription Typing. *Psychological Bulletin, 99*(3), 303–319. DOI: 10.1037/0033-2909.99.3.303 39, 40

Salvucci, D., & Taatgen, N. (2008). Threaded cognition: an integrated theory of concurrent multi-tasking. *Psychological Review, 115*(1), 101–130. DOI: 10.1037/0033-295X.115.1.101 25

Sauer, J., Wastell, D. G., Robert, G., Hockey, J., & Earle, F. (2003). Performance in a complex multiple-task environment during a laboratory-based simulation of occasional night work. *Human Factors: The Journal of the Human Factors and Ergonomics Society*, *45*(4), 657–670. DOI: 10.1518/hfes.45.4.657.27090 26

Schmidt, R. A., & Bjork, R. A. (1992). New conceptualizations of practice: Common principles in three paradigms suggest new concepts for training. *Psychological science*, *3*(4), 207–217. DOI: 10.1111/j.1467-9280.1992.tb00029.x 78

Schmidt, R. A., Zelaznik, H., Hawkins, B., Frank, J. S., & Quinn Jr, J. T. (1979). Motor-output variability: a theory for the accuracy of rapid motor acts. *Psychological review*, *86*(5), 415. DOI: 10.1037/0033-295X.86.5.415 34

Schumacher, E., Lauber, E., Glass, J., Zurbriggen, E., Gmeindl, L., Kieras, D., et al. (1999). Concurrent response-selection processes in dual-task performance: evidence for adaptive executive control of task scheduling. *Journal of Experimental psychology*, *25*(3), 791–814. DOI: 10.1037/0096-1523.25.3.791 36, 41, 42, 43, 44

Simon, H. A. (1957). *Administrative behavior* (Vol. 4). Cambridge Univ Press. 52, 55

Simon, H. A. (1992). What is an 'explanation' of behavior? *Psychological Science*, *3*(3), 150. DOI: 10.1111/j.1467-9280.1992.tb00017.x 46

Singh, S., Lewis, R., Barto, A., & Sorg, J. (2010). Intrinsically motivated reinforcement learning: An evolutionary perspective. *IEEE Transactions on Autonomous Mental Development*. DOI: 10.1109/TAMD.2010.2051031 4

Smith, M. R., Lewis, R. L., Howes, A., Chu, A., & Green, C. (2008). More than 8,192 Ways to Skin a Cat : Modeling Behavior in Multidimensional Strategy Spaces. In B. C. Love, K. McRae, & V. M. Sloutsky (Eds.), *Proceedings of the 30th annual conference of the cognitive science society* (pp. 1441–1446). Austin, Tx: Cognitive Science Society. 5, 10, 44, 65

Smith, S. M., & Blankenship, S. E. (1991). Incubation and the persistence of fixation in problem solving. *The American journal of psychology*, 61–87. DOI: 10.2307/1422851 25

Sorkin, R. D., & Dai, H. (1994). Signal Detection Analysis of the Ideal Group. *Organizational Behavior and Human Decision Processes*, *60*(1), 1–13. DOI: 10.1006/obhd.1994.1072 18

Sorkin, R. D., Hays, C. J., & West, R. (2001). Signal-Detection Analysis of Group Decision Making. *Psychological Review*, *108*(I), 183–203. DOI: 10.1037/0033-295X.108.1.183 18

Sorkin, R. D., Kantowitz, B. H., & Kantowitz, S. C. (1988). Likelihood alarm displays. *Human Factors: The Journal of the Human Factors and Ergonomics Society*, *30*(4), 445–459. DOI: 10.1177/001872088803000406 18

Sorkin, R. D., West, R., & Robinson, D. E. (1998). Group performance depends on the majority rule. *Psychological Science*, *9*(6), 456–463. DOI: 10.1111/1467-9280.00085 18

Sorkin, R. D., & Woods, D. D. (1985). Systems with human monitors: A signal detection analysis. *Human-Computer Interaction*, *1*(1), 49–75. DOI: 10.1207/s15327051hci0101_2 18, 19, 81

Sparrow, B., Liu, J., & Wegner, D. M. (2011). Google effects on memory: Cognitive consequences of having information at our fingertips. *science*, *333*(6043), 776–778. DOI: 10.1126/science.1207745 3, 62

Stephens, D. W., & Krebs, J. R. (1986). *Foraging theory*. Princeton Univ Press. 7, 8, 9, 28

Stevens, J. R., Volstorf, J., Schooler, L. J., & Rieskamp, J. (2011). Forgetting constrains the emergence of cooperative decision strategies. *Frontiers in Psychology*, *1*(January), 1–12. DOI: 10.3389/fpsyg.2010.00235 73, 74

Styles, E. (2006). *The psychology of attention*. Psychology Press. 25

Suchman, L. A. (1987). *Plans and situated actions: the problem of human-machine communication.* Cambridge university press. 2

Sutton, R. S., & Barto, A. G. (1998). *Reinforcement learning: an introduction*. MIT Press. 7

Swets, J., Tanner Jr, W., & Birdsall, T. (1961). Decision processes in perception. *Psychological Review*, *68*(5), 301–340. DOI: 10.1037/h0040547 7, 12, 75, 81

Tollinger, I., Lewis, R., McCurdy, M., Tollinger, P., Vera, A., Howes, A., et al. (2005). Supporting Efficient Development of Cognitive Models at Multiple Skill Levels : Exploring Recent Advances in Constraint-based modeling. In *Proceedings of the sigchi conference on human factors in computing systems* (pp. 411–420). ACM. DOI: 10.1145/1054972.1055029 10, 65

Toomim, M., Kriplean, T., Pörtner, C., & Landay, J. (2011). Utility of human-computer interactions: Toward a science of preference measurement. In *Proceedings of the 2011 annual conference on human factors in computing systems* (pp. 2275–2284). DOI: 10.1145/1978942.1979277 5

Trommershäuser, J., Maloney, L. T., & Landy, M. S. (2003). Statistical decision theory and trade-offs in the control of motor response. *Spatial vision*, *16*(3-4), 255–75. DOI: 10.1163/156856803322467527 32, 36, 75

Trommershäuser, J., Maloney, L. T., & Landy, M. S. (2008). Decision making, movement planning and statistical decision theory. *Trends in Cognitive Sciences*(July), 291–297. DOI: 10.1016/j.tics.2008.04.010 32

Trommershäuser, J., Maloney, L. T., & Landy, M. S. (2009). The Expected Utility of Movement. *Brain*, 95–111. 32

Vera, A., Howes, A., McCurdy, M., & Lewis, R. L. (2004). A constraint satisfaction approach to predicting skilled interactive cognition. In *Proceedings of the sigchi conference on human factors in computing systems* (pp. 121–128). DOI: 10.1145/985692.985708 10, 42, 65

Waldron, S. M., Patrick, J., Duggan, G. B., Banbury, S., & Howes, A. (2008). Designing information fusion for the encoding of visual–spatial information. *Ergonomics*, *51*(6), 775–797. DOI: 10.1080/00140130701811933 10

Welford, A. T., Norris, A. H., & Shock, N. W. (1969). Speed and accuracy of movement and their changes with age. *Acta psychologica*, *30*, 3–15. DOI: 10.1016/0001-6918(69)90034-1 31, 34, 35

Whittaker, S., Bellotti, V., & Cwizdka, J. (2007). CD Everything through Email. *Personal Information Management*, 167. 63

Whittaker, S., Bellotti, V., & Gwizdka, J. (2006). Email in personal information management. *Communications of the ACM*, *49*(1), 68–73. DOI: 10.1145/1107458.1107494 10, 63

Wilke, A., Hutchinson, J., Todd, P. M., & Czienskowski, U. (2009). Fishing for the right words: Decision rules for human foraging behavior in internal search tasks. *Cognitive Science*, *33*(3), 497–529. DOI: 10.1111/j.1551-6709.2009.01020.x 27

Wilkinson, S. C., Reader, W., & Payne, S. J. (2012). Adaptive browsing: Sensitivity to time pressure and task difficulty. *International Journal of Human-Computer Studies*, *70*(1), 14–25. DOI: 10.1016/j.ijhcs.2011.08.003 26, 52, 56, 57, 58

Winkler, I., Jonas, K., & Rudolph, U. (2008). On the Usefulness of Memory Skills in Social Interactions Modifying the Iterated Prisoner's Dilemma. *Journal of Conflict Resolution*, *52*(3), 375–384. DOI: 10.1177/0022002707312606 73

Wolfe, M. B. W., Schreiner, M. E., Rehder, B., Laham, D., Foltz, P. W., Kintsch, W., et al. (1998). Learning from text: Matching readers and texts by latent semantic analysis. *Discourse Processes*, *25*(2-3), 309–336. DOI: 10.1080/01638539809545030 53, 54, 56

Wu, C., & Liu, Y. (2004). Modeling Human Transcription Typing with Queuing Network-Model Human Processor (QN-MHP). In *Proceedings of the human factors and ergonomics society annual meeting* (Vol. 48, pp. 381–385). DOI: 10.1177/154193120404800323 39

Wu, C., & Liu, Y. (2008). Queuing network modeling of transcription typing. *ACM Transactions on Computer-Human Interaction (TOCHI)*, *15*(1), 6. DOI: 10.1145/1352782.1352788 39

Young, R. M., & MacLean, A. (1988). Choosing between methods: analysing the user's decision space in terms of schemas and linear models. In *Proceedings of the sigchi conference on human factors in computing systems* (pp. 139–143). DOI: 10.1145/57167.57190 7

Zhang, J., & Norman, D. (1994). Representations in distributed cognitive tasks. *Cognitive Science*, *18*(1), 87–122. DOI: 10.1207/s15516709cog1801_3 3, 63

Authors' Biographies

STEPHEN PAYNE

Stephen Payne is professor of human-centric systems in the Department of Computer Science at the University of Bath. Before moving to Bath, Payne was a Professor of Psychology in Cardiff University and (briefly) a Professor in Manchester Business School. Previously he worked at IBM T.J. Watson Research Center. Payne has worked on cognitive approaches to Human-Computer Interaction since his PhD on Task-Action Grammars, awarded in 1985.

ANDREW HOWES

Andrew Howes is professor of Human-Computer Interaction in the School of Computer Science at the University of Birmingham, UK. He has previously held posts as Professor of Cognitive Systems at Manchester Business School, University of Manchester, and before that as Senior Lecturer in the School of Psychology at the University of Cardiff. Howes is interested in computational theories of the strategies that people choose given psychological constraints.

Printed in the United States
by Baker & Taylor Publisher Services